THREE KINGS

Mark E. Petersen

THREE KINGS

of Israel

Deseret Book Company
Salt Lake City, Utah
1980

© 1980 Deseret Book Company
All rights reserved
Printed in the United States of America

Library of Congress Cataloging in Publication Data

Petersen, Mark E
    Three kings of Israel.

        Includes index.
        1. Saul, King of Israel. 2. David, King of
Israel. 3. Solomon, King of Israel. 4. Bible.
O.T–Biography. 5. Jews–Kings and rulers–
Biography. I. Title.
BS579.K5P47   222'.40922 [B]   80-36697
ISBN O-87747-829-5

CONTENTS

PART I
THEY HAVE REJECTED ME!

"And ye shall cry out in that day because of your king which ye shall have chosen you; and the Lord will not hear you in that day."
(1 Samuel 8:18.)

Chapter One

GLORY, THEN ECLIPSE

Israel's greatest kings were Saul, David, and Solomon. Each rose like a brilliant meteor in a clear sky. Each had his setting in tragedy. Each was favored of the Lord in the beginning of his reign and rose to enviable heights. But each sinned before God and man, and lost his high status with the Lord.

One disobeyed the Almighty from the early part of his regime. He was headstrong, willful, and overconfident. Although rejected by the Lord early in his reign, he carried on defiantly for years. He wove for himself a mesh of sin and failure. As the entangling web closed about him, he sought escape through the occult. Against his own law, he consulted one "who peeps and mutters." The witch left him in the depths of despair. He came to an ignominious end on the battlefield, but not in honorable combat.

The next was a "man after God's own heart." He became a great and victorious king who freed his people from all their enemies and established a powerful monarchy in Jerusalem. At the height of his career he succumbed to moral temptation. That act led to a worse sin. He resorted to murder as a means of disposing of Bathsheba's husband, whom he placed in the midst of battle, where he was killed according to the monarch's own preconceived scheme. The woman was then taken into the royal palace as a plural wife of the sovereign.

So the Lord condemned this king also, and as the scripture indicates, "he hath fallen from his exaltation" even though he had been well beloved of Jehovah. (D&C 132:39.)

The third, blessed above all other men at the beginning of his reign, achieved a greatness and a fame unknown before or since in Israel. He was given wisdom by the revelation of the Holy Spirit, and was showered with wealth and power also as gifts of heaven. The brilliance of his court attracted the elite of the world, who came in pilgrimages to see his dazzling kingdom and to bask in his wise judgment and inspired discernment.

But he fell, too. Love for forbidden women was his ruin. This seductive connubial affection eclipsed his relationship with God, whom he not only disregarded, but also seriously offended by his repeated disobedience. He raised up pagan shrines and graven images for his heathen wives and brought idolatry into his kingdom in the face of the Lord's specific commandment against it. He put God aside, and the Lord reacted in kind.

The lives of these three kings provide a striking lesson in both obedience and rebellion. The prophet Samuel epitomized it when he told Saul: "To obey is better than sacrifice, and to hearken than the fat of rams." (1 Samuel 15:22.)

This principle applies to individuals, families, and even to nations. It was held before the ancient Israelites in Palestine down through the centuries, but they never were disposed to accept the lesson nor to profit by it. It was taught to the ancient Americans, but they went their own way to eventual destruction at Cumorah. And it is taught to us today.

Selfishness and personal desire can displace love of God. When faith is lost, the insatiable appetite of personal desire takes over and obedience ceases to exist. Then comes the night when no man can work.

Chapter Two

KINGS VS. PROPHETS

The ancient Israelites had one dreadful enemy. It was not the Hittites, nor the Phoenicians, nor even the Philistines. It was their own overpowering and misguided yearning to be like other nations.

Their neighbors in Palestine had two major attractions. One was that they had kings to govern them, with all the pomp and ceremony of the royal courts. The other was their sensual idolatrous religion. Many in Israel wanted both.

The only government the Twelve Tribes had known since leaving Egypt, where they were slaves to Pharaoh, was rule by revelation through a living prophet.

First it was Moses who led them by divine direction. Through him God brought them out of Egypt and gave them guidance during their forty years' travel in the wilderness. It was the Lord who fed them there, miraculously, and provided them with both shelter and raiment. It was the Almighty who gave them the Ten Commandments and the law of Moses for their standard of conduct.

Moses, as the Lord's spokesman, was their governor, their guide, their arbiter, their great teacher and protector. But above all else, he was a prophet.

When Moses passed on, Joshua was named to lead the tribes in the same pattern of government. Chosen of heaven by revelation from God, he also became a prophet.

With his appointment, the Almighty promised this new leader: "As I was with Moses, so I will be with thee: I will not fail thee, nor forsake thee." (Joshua 1:5.)

But then the Lord added a caution, indicating that complete obedience must be the basis of Joshua's success. So the divine word continued: "Be thou strong and very courageous, that thou mayest observe to do according to all the law, which Moses my servant commanded thee: turn not from it to the right hand or to the left, that thou mayest prosper whithersoever thou goest." (Joshua 1:7.)

The people accepted the leadership of Joshua on that basis. They willingly recognized the divine principle by which he was made their governor, and pledged to him: "According as we hearkened unto Moses in all things, so will we hearken unto thee: only the Lord thy God be with thee, as he was with Moses." (Joshua 1:17.)

Then and there they accepted this high principle of government by revelation and solemnly promised to be loyal to their new prophet-leader. They fully expected that as Moses had led them by the power of God, so would Joshua; they prayed, "Only the Lord thy God be with thee, as he was with Moses."

When Joshua's life neared its end, he gathered the people together and reminded them of their covenant, pleading with them to serve their heavenly Benefactor who had brought them out of Egyptian slavery and into the Promised Land, which in those days did "flow with milk and honey." The land was fertile and highly productive, and would continue so only if Israel obeyed the Lord.

The aging prophet knew that many had forgotten the Almighty and had turned to the false gods of their neighbors. So he remonstrated with them: "If ye forsake the Lord, and serve strange gods, then he will turn and do you hurt, and consume you." (Joshua 24:20.)

He continued with his exhortation: "If it seem evil unto you to serve the Lord, choose you this day whom ye will serve; whether the gods which your fathers served that were on the other side of the flood [the river Jordan, which was at flood stage when the tribes crossed it as they came into Canaan], or the gods of the Amorites, in whose land ye dwell: but as for me and my house, we will serve the Lord." (Joshua 24:15.)

This is one of the best remembered passages in the Bible.

For a time the people responded, turned from their evil ways, and pledged: "The Lord our God will we serve, and his voice will we obey. So Joshua made a covenant with the people that day, and set them a statute and an ordinance in Shechem." (Joshua 24:24-25.)

Thus firmly was the principle of government by prophecy re-confirmed among the Twelve Tribes.

But after the death of Joshua the people soon forgot their promises and began to stray into the forbidden paths against which they had been so sharply warned.

Two great challenges faced them. One was their tempting neighbors. Israel envied both their kings and their loose way of life. The other was that no strong successor had been provided for them after Joshua's death. For a time the tribal leaders took over, but they were local in their influence and proved inadequate to defend Israel against her hostile neighbors.

During this period "judges" were raised up by the Lord to "fill the gap." Of these judges the *Bible Companion* explains:

"The word 'judge' is a misnomer; it gives a false picture of his function. A truer description is given by the word 'deliverer.' The judges had no legal status, and only occasionally were they called upon to give legal decisions. Their main purpose was to 'save' Israel by organizing a revolt against the oppressors." (William Neal, ed. [New York: McGraw-Hill, 1960], p. 348.)

As a crisis developed, a "deliverer" would arise in Israel, sometimes being self-appointed. Generally there was no united effort behind him, so that success, if any, was limited.

This was a period of confusion for Israel, with no strong prophet-figure at their head and with much temptation from their neighbor nations, who flaunted before them the pomp of their kings as well as the seduction of their idolatrous religions.

Chapter Three

THE REIGN OF THE JUDGES

When Joshua died and Israel was left without a central government, her priests still labored in the tabernacle, elders discussed religious matters, and occasionally a prophet served the people.

But there was no basic authority recognized by all the tribes, no overall direction for the nation. As the writer of the book of Judges comments at various times: ''In those days there was no king in Israel: every man did that which was right in his own eyes.'' (Judges 21:25.)

The tribes still fought against the Canaanites, but they also fought among themselves, with thousands of their own brethren being killed on both sides. For example, in one battle between the tribe of Benjamin and others in Israel, ''the children of Benjamin came forth out of Gibeah, and destroyed down to the ground of the Israelites that day twenty and two thousand men.'' (Judges 20:21.)

In another battle ''the Lord smote Benjamin before Israel: and the children of Israel destroyed of the Benjamites that day twenty and five thousand and an hundred men: all these drew the sword.'' (Judges 20:35.)

The combined strength of Benjamin and the rest of Israel was given as four hundred thousand ''men that drew sword: all these were men of war.'' (Judges 20:17.)

A feud developed between the people of Ephraim and the tribe of Jephthah. Obtaining help from Gilead, Jephthah attacked his brethren ''and there fell at that time of the Ephraimites forty and two thousand.'' (Judges 12:6.)

The Israelites continued their wars against the Canaanites but the Lord never allowed them to wipe out their enemies entirely or to overcome them. He intended to use Canaan as a chastening influence upon his people.

''Now the children of Judah had fought against Jerusalem,

and had taken it, and smitten it with the edge of the sword, and set the city on fire.'' (Judges 1:8.) It was later lost again. It will be remembered that Joshua never did capture that city, although he fought successfully against its king in another battle.

Other cities now fell in these tribal campaigns. ''And the Lord was with Judah; and he drave out the inhabitants of the mountain; but could not drive out the inhabitants of the valley, because they had chariots of iron.'' (Judges 1:19.)

The record then indicates that all of the tribes occasionally fought the Canaanites, but at no time was the enemy destroyed or conquered. The Lord had said: ''I will not drive them out from before you; but they shall be as thorns in your sides, and their gods shall be a snare unto you.'' (Judges 2:3.)

And why would the Lord do this? Because of the apostate and unclean practices of the Israelites!

A new generation had grown up since the days of Joshua, and they ''knew not the Lord, nor yet the works which he had done for Israel. And the children of Israel did evil in the sight of the Lord, and served Baalim: And they forsook the Lord God of their fathers, which brought them out of the land of Egypt, and followed other gods, of the gods of the people that were round about them, and bowed themselves unto them, and provoked the Lord to anger. And they forsook the Lord, and served Baal and Ashtaroth.

''And the anger of the Lord was hot against Israel, and he delivered them into the hands of spoilers that spoiled them, and he sold them into the hands of their enemies round about, so that they could not any longer stand before their enemies.

''Whithersoever they went out, the hand of the Lord was against them for evil, as the Lord had said, and as the Lord had sworn unto them: and they were greatly distressed.'' (Judges 2:10-15.)

But the Lord has infinite patience. He had pledged to Moses and Joshua that he would bring his people into the land of milk and honey, which Palestine was at that time, and had promised them great prosperity, even with peace, if they would serve him. In spite of their apostate ways, he still endeavored to keep his promise to Abraham by saving this stubborn people from themselves.

The Lord determined upon a new form of government. Whether he had in mind an approach to some kind of democratic rule is not clear, but from among the people he "raised up judges" as deliverers and leaders in their battles, but also to provide some semblance of centralized authority.

Some of these judges reigned for as long as forty years, and under their rule peace prevailed at times. Some of the judges were fighters, too, great leaders in the battles of the Israelites, and in many instances they won significant victories.

"And yet they would not hearken unto their judges, but they went a whoring after other gods, and bowed themselves unto them: they turned quickly out of the way which their fathers walked in, obeying the commandments of the Lord; but they did not so. And when the Lord raised them up judges, then the Lord was with the judge, and delivered them out of the hand of their enemies."

But when a judge died, and apparently before his successor was named, "they returned, and corrupted themselves more than their fathers, in following other gods to serve them, and to bow down unto them; they ceased not from their own doings, nor from their stubborn way."

The anger of the Lord "was hot against Israel; and he said, Because that this people hath transgressed my covenant which I commanded their fathers, and have not hearkened unto my voice; I also will not henceforth drive out any from before them of the nations which Joshua left when he died: That through them I may prove Israel, whether they will keep the way of the Lord to walk therein, as their fathers did keep it, or not. Therefore the Lord left those nations, without driving them out hastily; neither delivered he them into the hand of Joshua." (Judges 2:16-23.)

To crown their evil deeds, Israelites now intermarried with the Canaanites, which again further angered the Lord.

"And the children of Israel dwelt among the Canaanites, Hittites, and Amorites, and Perizzites, and Hivites, and Jebusites: And they took their daughters to be their wives, and gave their daughters to their sons, and served their gods.

"And the children of Israel did evil in the sight of the Lord, and forgat the Lord their God, and served Baalim and the groves.

"Therefore the anger of the Lord was hot against Israel, and he sold them into the hand of Chushan-rishathaim king of Mesopotamia: and the children of Israel served Chushan-rishathaim eight years.

"And when the children of Israel cried unto the Lord, the Lord raised up a deliverer to the children of Israel, who delivered them, even Othniel the son of Kenaz, Caleb's younger brother.

"And the Spirit of the Lord came upon him, and he judged Israel, and went out to war: and the Lord delivered Chushan-rishathaim king of Mesopotamia into his hand; and his hand prevailed against Chushan-rishathaim.

"And the land had rest forty years. And Othniel the son of Kenaz died." (Judges 3:5-11.)

This became a pattern in Israel for many years: sin and idolatry, followed by distress and repentance. Then the Lord would come to their aid, until once again they would go astray. It seemed like an endless cycle.

This was a sad period for the people of promise. But from time to time the Lord continued to raise up strong men—and one mighty woman—to deliver them and to govern them.

One of these men was Gideon, that valiant defender of their lands and faithful servant of God. Another was Samson, who fought with superhuman physical strength, yet was a weakling in the hands of a clever woman. Samson judged Israel "in the days of the Philistines twenty years." (Judges 15:20.)

Their great female deliverer was Deborah, a prophetess. She was a mother in Israel, the wife of Lapidoth, "and the children of Israel came up to her for judgment."

With the aid of a faithful lieutenant named Barak she fearlessly defeated an enemy army that had nine hundred chariots made of iron "from Herosheth of the Gentiles." Following her victory Deborah sang a hymn to the Lord, which included these words: "let all thine enemies perish, O Lord: but let them that love him be as the sun when he goeth forth in his might." Under her rule, the scripture says, "the land had rest forty years." (Judges 4, 5.)

After decades of vacillating between the Lord and the heathen gods, and after years of uncertain rule on the part of the judges, the people became more and more rebellious.

In the midst of this unrest, Samuel was born. He became both a prophet and a judge, but by this time the people paid little heed to either prophets or judges, and became steeped in idolatry. They wanted to be like their neighboring nations, with kings instead of either prophets or judges and with freedom to worship any gods they pleased. It was a tragic turning point in the history of ancient Israel. It was the opening wedge of their ultimate apostasy.

The surrounding nations boasted of their kings. The pomp of the royal courts was in striking contrast to the simplicity of the lives and homes of the Lord's prophets. The heathen glamour, both in their kingly courts and in their pagan temples, intrigued Israel despite the displeasure of Jehovah.

When they ignored the Lord and worshipped false gods, they lost their battles with the Canaanites because the Lord would not deliver them in their sins. They saw that their enemies were led by warrior kings in battle, and they began to feel that kings were an essential ingredient of victory.

The people came to Samuel, now both prophet and judge, and demanded a king for themselves. They wanted to end the rule of the judges.

The Lord spoke to Samuel in no uncertain terms, warning both him and the people against this change of affairs.

"And Samuel told all the words of the Lord unto the people that asked of him a king.

"And he said, This will be the manner of the king that shall reign over you: He will take your sons, and appoint them for himself, for his chariots, and to be his horsemen; and some shall run before his chariots.

"And he will appoint him captains over thousands, and captains over fifties; and will set them to ear his ground, and to reap his harvest, and to make his instruments of war, and instruments of his chariots.

"And he will take your daughters to be confectionaries, and to be cooks, and to be bakers.

"And he will take your fields, and your vineyards, and your oliveyards, even the best of them, and give them to his servants.

"And he will take the tenth of your seed, and of your vineyards, and give to his officers, and to his servants.

"And he will take your menservants, and your maidservants,

and your goodliest young men, and your asses, and put them to his work.

"He will take the tenth of your sheep: and ye shall be his servants.

"And ye shall cry out in that day because of your king which ye shall have chosen you; and the Lord will not hear you in that day." (1 Samuel 8:10-18.)

His warnings were to no avail. "The people refused to obey the voice of Samuel; and they said, Nay; but we will have a king over us; That we also may be like all the nations; and that our king may judge us, and go out before us, and fight our battles." (1 Samuel 8:19-20.)

This attitude of rebellion was heightened by the deadly influence of the heathen religions that many now adopted. One form of apostasy led to another, and Israel served "the strange gods of Ashtaroth and Baalim," which was a severe affront to the Lord.

So the Israelites now had reached the point where they were willing to discard their prophet leader and adopt the worldliness that surrounded them.

Samuel was deeply grieved, but the Lord said to him: "They have not rejected thee, but they have rejected me, that I should not reign over them."(1 Samuel 8:7.)

"Samuel heard all the words of the people, and he rehearsed them in the ears of the Lord. And the Lord said to Samuel, Hearken unto their voice, and make them a king." (1 Samuel 8:21-22.)

The Lord would not compel anyone, not even these recalcitrant Israelites. He would not upset his principle of free agency for any reason. When the people turned against him in the face of his repeated persuasion, the Lord simply let them go.

As they came out of Egypt in Moses' day, Israel was promised that she could become the greatest nation on earth if she would serve the Lord. (Deuteronomy 28:1.) But now the people rejected this opportunity. To become like their neighbors was more desirable. Their choice ultimately led them into captivity and despair.

Chapter Four

THE MISUSE
OF POWER

The experience of Israel with kings who ruled over them in Palestine was in sharp contrast to the reign of the great kings of ancient America. This, of course, was because the righteous kings described in the Book of Mormon were prophet-kings, governors like Moses and Joshua, although neither of these two great personalities was made a king. That was not the Lord's way for Palestine.

One of the greatest of the prophet-kings of America was Benjamin, who partook of nothing like the pomp of the Palestinian rulers. He lived a common life, even worked with his hands to sustain himself and his family.

Like him was his son Mosiah. Mosiah, however, recognized the dangers in kingship, even as did Samuel, and strongly warned his people against the evils that a wicked king could bring upon them. Said he:

"Now I say unto you, that because all men are not just it is not expedient that ye should have a king or kings to rule over you.

"For behold, how much iniquity doth one wicked king cause to be committed, yea, and what great destruction!

"Yea, remember king Noah, his wickedness and his abominations, and also the wickedness and abominations of his people. Behold what great destruction did come upon them; and also because of their iniquities they were brought into bondage.

"And were it not for the interposition of their all-wise Creator, and this because of their sincere repentance, they must unavoidably remain in bondage until now.

"But behold, he did deliver them because they did humble themselves before him; and because they cried mightily unto him he did deliver them out of bondage; and thus doth the Lord work with his power in all cases among the children of men, extending the arm of mercy towards them that put their trust in him.

"And behold, now I say unto you, ye cannot dethrone an iniquitous king save it be through much contention, and the shedding of much blood.

"For behold, he has his friends in iniquity, and he keepeth his guards about him; and he teareth up the laws of those who have reigned in righteousness before him; and he trampleth under his feet the commandments of God;

"And he enacteth laws, and sendeth them forth among his people, yea, laws after the manner of his own wickedness; and whosoever doth not obey his laws he causeth to be destroyed; and whosoever doth rebel against him he will send his armies against them to war, and if he can he will destroy them; and thus an unrighteous king doth pervert the ways of all righteousness.

"And now behold I say unto you, it is not expedient that such abominations should come upon you.

"Therefore, choose you by the voice of this people, judges, that ye may be judged according to the laws which have been given you by our fathers, which are correct, and which were given them by the hand of the Lord.

"Now it is not common that the voice of the people desireth anything contrary to that which is right; but it is common for the lesser part of the people to desire that which is not right; therefore this shall ye observe and make it your law—to do your business by the voice of the people.

"And if the time comes that the voice of the people doth choose iniquity, then is the time that the judgments of God will come upon you; yea, then is the time he will visit you with great destruction even as he has hitherto visited this land.

"And now if ye have judges, and they do not judge you according to the law which has been given, ye can cause that they may be judged of a higher judge.

"If your higher judges do not judge righteous judgments, ye shall cause that a small number of your lower judges should be gathered together, and they shall judge your higher judges, according to the voice of the people.

"And I command you to do these things in the fear of the Lord; and I command you to do these things, and that ye have no king; and if these people commit sins and iniquities they shall be answered upon their own heads.

"For behold I say unto you, the sins of many people have been caused by the iniquities of their kings; therefore their iniquities are answered upon the heads of their kings.

"And now I desire that this inequality should be no more in this land, especially among this my people; but I desire that this land be a land of liberty, and every man may enjoy his rights and privileges alike, so long as the Lord sees fit that we may live and inherit the land, yea, even as long as any of our posterity remains upon the face of the land. . . .

"And now it came to pass, after king Mosiah had sent these things forth among the people they were convinced of the truth of his words.

"Therefore they relinquished their desires for a king, and became exceedingly anxious that every man should have an equal chance throughout all the land; yea, and every man expressed a willingness to answer for his own sins.

"Therefore, it came to pass that they assembled themselves together in bodies throughout the land, to cast in their voices concerning who should be their judges, to judge them according to the law which had been given them; and they were exceedingly rejoiced because of the liberty which had been granted unto them." (Mosiah 29:16-32, 37-39.)

So freedom was established in America. Kings were abolished and the government rested with the voice of the people.

But in Palestine, in the days of Samuel, the Israelites went the opposite way. They demanded a king against the will of the Lord and despite all the divine warnings to the contrary. The king they chose, and others to follow, led them into war, destruction, and eventual subjection to their enemies.

PART II
KING SAUL:
SON OF KISH-THE BENJAMITE

*"To obey is better than sacrifice,
and to hearken than the fat of rams.
For rebellion is as the sin of witchcraft,
and stubbornness is as iniquity and idolatry."
(1 Samuel 15:22-23.)*

Chapter Five

SAUL IS CHOSEN KING

Although the people rejected the counsel of the Lord in demanding a king, the Almighty nevertheless endeavored to make the best of the situation.

Since the people had demanded a new ruler, the Lord determined to give them the best man available for such a high place, and to enable him by special blessings to conduct a proper reign. He would give the king "a new heart," bless him with his Holy Spirit, and even confer the gift of prophecy upon him. What more could God do?

Saul, the son of Kish, of the tiny tribe of Benjamin, was selected by the Lord for this position. The scripture says that he was a "choice young man, and a goodly: and there was not among the children of Israel a goodlier person than he." (1 Samuel 9:1-2.)

Saul had the desirable physique, too, for he stood head and shoulders above all other men. He was not a giant in the sense that Goliath was, for Goliath stood over ten feet high. But Saul was much taller than any other man in Israel.

At this time the tribes were under the domination of the Philistines. Because they had no central government and even fought among themselves, they had no united strength to resist the incursions of the enemy.

When the Lord spoke to Samuel about elevating Saul, he made it clear that the objective of the new king must be to "save my people out of the hand of the Philistines: for I have looked upon my people, because their cry is come unto me." (1 Samuel 9:16.)

The infinite patience of the Lord in dealing with Israel in the face of their constant disobedience can only excite wonder and amazement. But he is God, and he had made covenants with Abraham, Moses, and Joshua to preserve his people. The Lord gave them constant opportunities to repent, and this was one of them.

Saul had a humble beginning. One day the asses of Kish, Saul's father, were lost. "And Kish said to Saul his son, Take now one of the servants with thee, and arise, go seek the asses." (1 Samuel 9:3.)

This Saul did, but although he and the servant searched the land from Mount Ephraim to Shalim, they could not find the animals. When they arrived at the land of Zuph, they decided to return home without them. Then it occurred to Saul that Samuel, the seer of the Lord, lived nearby. He decided to ask Samuel to tell him by inspiration where to find the animals. When they arrived in the city, Samuel came out to meet them.

"Now the Lord had told Samuel in his ear a day before Saul came, saying,

"To morrow about this time I will send thee a man out of the land of Benjamin, and thou shalt anoint him to be captain over my people Israel, that he may save my people out of the hand of the Philistines: for I have looked upon my people, because their cry is come unto me.

"And when Samuel saw Saul, the Lord said unto him, Behold the man whom I spake to thee of! this same shall reign over my people.

"Then Saul drew near to Samuel in the gate, and said, Tell me, I pray thee, where the seer's house is.

"And Samuel answered Saul, and said, I am the seer."

Samuel invited Saul into his house and had his cook prepare a sumptious feast for the occasion. Thirty friends also were invited in. Addressing his guest of honor, Samuel said, referring to their desire for a king, "On whom is all the desire of Israel? Is it not on thee, and on all thy father's house?"

Saul was very humble about the matter and said, "Am not I a Benjamite, of the smallest of the tribes of Israel? and my family the least of all the families of the tribe of Benjamin? wherefore then speakest thou so to me?"

Samuel brought Saul and his servant into his parlor "and made them sit in the chiefest place among them that were bidden, which were about thirty persons." (1 Samuel 9:15-22.)

This is an interesting passage. For one thing, in his own home

Samuel gave a feast in honor of Saul's appointment as king, and invited thirty people to attend. But also it is shown that Samuel lived in a city, he had a large house with a parlor that would accommodate thirty guests, and he had a cook.

Those who indicate that all the prophets were desert nomads living in tents are not acquainted with the facts. Samuel, of course, was both prophet and judge. In this latter position he may have been given certain emoluments that raised his standard of living above the ordinary.

"And Samuel said unto the cook, Bring the portion which I gave thee, of which I said unto thee, Set it by thee.

"And the cook took up the shoulder, and that which was upon it, and set it before Saul. And Samuel said, Behold that which is left! set it before thee, and eat: for unto this time hath it been kept for thee since I said, I have invited the people. So Saul did eat with Samuel that day."

Samuel "communed with Saul upon the top of the house," the record says, indicating that his confidential talk with him was completely private. Then they arose and "went out both of them, he and Samuel, abroad.

"And as they were going down to the end of the city, Samuel said to Saul, Bid the servant pass on before us, (and he passed on,) but stand thou still a while, that I may shew thee the word of God." (1 Samuel 9:23-27.)

After the servant had gone on ahead, Samuel took a vial of oil and poured it on Saul's head, kissed him, and said, "Is it not because the Lord hath anointed thee to be captain over his inheritance?" Then he gave Saul a series of signs by which he could know that his being anointed king was the Lord's will, saying:

"When thou art departed from me to day, then thou shalt find two men by Rachel's sepulchre in the border of Benjamin at Zelzah; and they will say unto thee, The asses which thou wentest to seek are found: and, lo, thy father hath left the care of the asses, and sorroweth for you, saying, What shall I do for my son?

"Then shalt thou go on forward from thence, and thou shalt come to the plain of Tabor, and there shall meet thee three men going up to God to Bethel, one carrying three kids, and another carrying three loaves of bread, and another carrying a bottle of wine:

"And they will salute thee, and give thee two loaves of bread; which thou shalt receive of their hands.

"After that thou shalt come to the hill of God, where is the garrison of the Philistines: and it shall come to pass, when thou art come thither to the city, that thou shalt meet a company of prophets coming down from the high place with a psaltery, and a tabret, and a pipe, and a harp, before them; and they shall prophesy:

"And the Spirit of the Lord will come upon thee, and thou shalt prophesy with them, and shalt be turned into another man.

"And let it be, when these signs are come unto thee, that thou do as occasion serve thee; for God is with thee." (1 Samuel 10:1-7.)

So every assurance was given the new king that the Lord would be with him, for God desired Saul to be successful in centralizing the government, uniting Israel, and freeing his chosen people from the enslaving hand of the Philistines.

Every opportunity for greatness was thus given to Saul, and a most important task was assigned to him. To help him to achieve this great work the Lord gave him "another heart," blessed him with his Spirit to inspire and guide him, and even conferred on him the gift of prophecy. It remained for Saul to measure up to his opportunity and "carry the torch of Israel." He possessed every requisite to become a great prophet-king if he would but truly obey the Lord.

The time now arrived for Samuel to announce Saul's appointment before all the people, so he called the tribes together at Mizpeh for this purpose. Before revealing Saul's selection, however, Samuel again upbraided the people for their departure from the ways of the Lord and told them in strong terms that by setting up this kingdom, they rejected the Lord, their king. Said he:

"Thus saith the Lord God of Israel, I brought up Israel out of Egypt, and delivered you out of the hand of the Egyptians, and out of the hand of all kingdoms, and of them that oppressed you:

"And ye have this day rejected your God, who himself saved you out of all your adversities and your tribulations; and ye have said unto him, Nay, but set a king over us. Now therefore present yourselves before the Lord by your tribes, and by your thousands."

He was ready to introduce the new king to the assembled multitude now, but when he looked for him, Saul could not be found. Samuel asked the Lord what had become of him, and the reply came back: ''Behold he hath hid himself among the stuff.''

Saul seemed amazingly timid at this point. But even so, after they had ''fetched him thence'' he stood before the tribes. He ''was higher than any of the people from his shoulders and upward.''

''And Samuel said to all the people, See ye him whom the Lord hath chosen, that there is none like him among all the people?'' Evidently he was not known to many, but his appearance was impressive for ''all the people shouted, and said, God save the king.'' Large physical stature apparently meant a good deal to them.

New hope came to enslaved Israel now. With the Lord ready to assist Saul in every righteous effort, and with Saul appearing to be obedient, the future seemed bright.

After the ceremonies, the Lord touched the hearts of the ''band of men'' who accompanied Saul to his home in Gibeah. Whether they constituted a bodyguard for the new king is not mentioned, but the record does show that ''the children of Belial'' protested against Saul at the ceremony, hated him, and asked, ''How shall this man save us?'' They despised him '' and brought him no presents,'' but Saul very wisely ''held his peace.'' (1 Samuel 10:9-27.)

The expression ''children of Belial'' usually means ''worthless, lawless fellows,'' according to Bible commentaries. The name Belial is also related to Satan and is applied elsewhere in scripture to ''all that is bad.''

These ''children of Belial'' who refused to sustain Saul evidently were merely a noisy minority like some we still have today, who are always against ''the establishment.''

Chapter Six

SAMUEL'S LAST WARNING

Although he had set up a king in Israel, Samuel continued to have misgivings. He knew that a wicked king could lead the nation astray.

How would Saul prove out under the honor and glory of his office? Would his humility continue? Would he remain faithful so that he could actually become the deliverer of Israel as the Lord had in mind? Or would Saul fail?

Samuel was well aware, too, of the unstable nature of the people, and realized that if they did not return wholeheartedly to the Lord, disaster could befall them, Saul or no Saul.

Shortly after appointing their king, Samuel called the tribes together and appealed to them once again to be loyal to the Lord, who was the source of their blessings. He had seen them vacillate in the past, going alternately from worship of the true God to adoration of the false deities of their wicked neighbors. And when affliction came upon them and the heathen gods failed to deliver them, he had seen them come weeping back to the Lord in all their immaturity. What of the future? Would Israel cease to be so childish and assume her true responsibility?

He was concerned over the rejection of the government through judges, but he knew the reason why. Most of the judges were inadequate and some corrupted the office, much to the disgust and distrust even of this vacillating people.

Samuel had appointed his own sons to the office of judge, and they were a great embarrassment to him. The elders of Israel came to Samuel complaining about them and said, "Behold, thou art old, and thy sons walk not in thy ways." The sons had "turned aside after lucre, and took bribes, and perverted judgment." Using this as a new reason for their demands, the elders said, "Now make us a king to judge us like all the nations." (1 Samuel 8:3,5.)

Samuel felt as if his own administration as judge was being questioned, and therefore he made an immediate defense of himself. He said: "I am old . . . and I have walked before you from my childhood unto this day. Behold, here I am: witness against me before the Lord, and before his annointed: whose ox have I taken? or whose ass have I taken? or whom have I defrauded? whom have I oppressed? or of whose hand have I received any bribe to blind mine eyes therewith? and I will restore it you. And they said, Thou hast not defrauded us, nor oppressed us, neither hast thou taken ought of any man's hand.

"And he said unto them, The Lord is witness against you, and his anointed [the king] is witness this day, that ye have not found ought in my hand. And they answered, He is witness."

Having thus established the integrity of his own administration, he now preached to them about the necessity of their being honest and obedient to the Lord under Saul's rule. He told of the instances in the past when the Lord had "delivered you out of the hand of your enemies on every side, and ye dwelled safe.

"And when ye saw that Nahash the king of the children of Ammon came against you, ye said unto me, Nay; but a king shall reign over us: when the Lord your God was your king.

"Now therefore behold the king whom ye have chosen, and whom ye have desired! and, behold, the Lord hath set a king over you. If ye will fear the Lord, and serve him, and obey his voice, and not rebel against the commandment of the Lord, then shall both ye and also the king that reigneth over you continue following the Lord your God:

"But if ye will not obey the voice of the Lord, but rebel against the commandment of the Lord, then shall the hand of the Lord be against you, as it was against your fathers."

He then reminded them of the Lord's love for them and his desire to bless them, and continued: "For the Lord will not forsake his people for his great name's sake: because it hath pleased the Lord to make you his people.Moreover as for me, God forbid that I should sin against the Lord in ceasing to pray for you: but I will teach you the good and the right way:

"Only fear the Lord, and serve him in truth with all your heart: for consider how great things he hath done for you.

"But if ye shall still do wickedly, ye shall be consumed, both ye and your king." (1 Samuel 12.)

Chapter Seven

SAUL'S FIRST VICTORY

Saul's administration began in a spirit of humility and obedience to the Lord. It held great promise.

The new king evidently was still at his father's home, herding the flocks and earning his own way without taxing the people. The Lord was with him, and Saul realized it.

One day as he was bringing a herd of livestock out of the field, he was met by some messengers from the town of Jabesh who told him that the Ammonites had encamped against their city, intending to destroy it and possibly take the populace captive.

The men of Jabesh in fear had said to the Ammonites, "Make a covenant with us, and we will serve thee." Nahash, the Ammonite leader, replied, "On this condition will I make a covenant with you, that I may thrust out all your right eyes, and lay it for a reproach upon all Israel."

The elders of Jabesh pleaded for time and hurriedly sent messengers to their new king, asking for protection. When Saul heard "the tidings of the men of Jabesh," the Spirit of God came upon him "and his anger was kindled greatly.

"And he took a yoke of oxen, and hewed them in pieces, and sent them throughout all the coasts of Israel by the hands of messengers, saying, Whosoever cometh not forth after Saul and after Samuel, so shall it be done unto his oxen. And the fear of the Lord fell on the people, and they came out with one consent.

"And when he numbered them in Bezek, the children of Israel were three hundred thousand, and the men of Judah thirty thousand.

"And they said unto the messengers that came, Thus shall ye say unto the men of Jabesh-gilead, To morrow, by that time the sun be hot, ye shall have help. And the messengers came and shewed it to the men of Jabesh; and they were glad."

The men from Jabesh now returned to their dealings with the Ammonites and said, "To morrow we will come out unto you, and ye shall do with us all that seemeth good unto you," as though they were capitulating to the demands of Nahash.

Saul quickly organized his troops into three divisions, and early in the morning they came against the Ammonites from three sides at once, completely routing the enemy forces and scattering them so that no two were left together.

This victory had an electrifying effect upon the Israelites, who now saw that indeed Saul could lead an army to victory, and that he could truly be their deliverer. They said, "Who is he that said, Shall Saul reign over us? bring the men, that we may put them to death."

But Saul wisely recognized that the victory came because of the Lord's intervention, and not from any military skill of his own nor from the strength of the people themselves. He was perfectly humble about the whole matter. Therefore he said: "There shall not a man be put to death this day: for to day the Lord hath wrought salvation in Israel."

Seeing that the attitude of the people was now so favorable toward Saul, although previously he was virtually an unknown to them, Samuel decided to have them reconfirm Saul's appointment. He said, "Come, and let us go to Gilgal, and renew the kingdom there.

"And all the people went to Gilgal; and there they made Saul king before the Lord in Gilgal; and there they sacrificed sacrifices of peace offerings before the Lord; and there Saul and all the men of Israel rejoiced greatly." (1 Samuel 11.)

Saul was now firmly established on the throne, not alone by the decree of Samuel, but by the full acceptance of the people themselves.

Chapter Eight

SAUL'S
FIRST MISTAKE

Within two years of the beginning of Saul's reign he made his first serious blunder. It came in a spirit of impatience, but also revealed a growing egotism in the new king's heart.

Some of the Israelites attacked a Philistine garrison in an outpost at Geba. When word reached the headquarters of the Philistines, they were enraged and decided at once on revenge. They amassed an army of thirty thousand chariots and six thousand horsemen and foot soldiers "as the sand which is on the sea shore in multitude: and they came up, and pitched in Michmash."

Although Saul had 330,000 fighting men, they were not mobilized and were in no way ready for combat. They were what we today speak of as "citizen soldiers": farmers and tradesmen, family men living in their own homes. So when this formidable force of Philistines arrived, ready for war, the Israelites were frightened and "hid themselves in caves, and in thickets, and in rocks, and in high places, and in pits."

Saul was in Gilgal, and some of the people came to him "trembling." He would not go out to battle without the aid of the Lord, so he asked Samuel to come and offer burnt offerings on the sacred altar as part of his appeal to the heavens.

Samuel replied that he could not come for seven days. Saul impatiently waited for the prophet, and when the seventh day came, with no sign of Samuel, the king determined to act without him.

It was not within the rights of the king to officiate in the ordinances of the Lord. That was for the ordained priests and prophets. Whether he felt that the "king can do no wrong" or whether he thought his authority to rule over Israel was all encompassing is not indicated in the scripture. But he foolishly determined to offer the sacrifice himself.

"And Saul said, Bring hither a burnt offering to me, and

peace offerings. And he offered the burnt offering.

"And it came to pass, that as soon as he had made an end of offering the burnt offering, behold, Samuel came; and Saul went out to meet him, that he might salute him.

"And Samuel said, What hast thou done? And Saul said, Because I saw that the people were scattered from me, and that thou camest not within the days appointed, and that the Philistines gathered themselves together at Michmash; Therefore said I, The Philistines will come down now upon me to Gilgal, and I have not made supplication unto the Lord: I forced myself therefore, and offered a burnt offering.

"And Samuel said to Saul, Thou hast done foolishly: thou hast not kept the commandment of the Lord thy God, which he commanded thee: for now would the Lord have established thy kingdom upon Israel for ever.

"But now thy kingdom shall not continue: the Lord hath sought him a man after his own heart, and the Lord hath commanded him to be captain over his people, because thou hast not kept that which the Lord commanded thee."

What a rebuke that was! And what a lesson for the new king!

"Now thy kingdom shall not continue: The Lord hath sought him a man after his own heart, and the Lord hath commanded him to be captain over his people." So Saul would be replaced! The Lord rejected him then and there.

And the reason: "Because thou hast not kept that which the Lord commanded thee." (1 Samuel 13:1-14.)

Here was a great lesson of what the Lord expects by way of obedience to his commandments. There was no room for vacillating on Saul's part. There was no "gray area" between the white and black of obedience and disobedience. Saul either obeyed the word of God or he did not. And in this unfortunate case, he did not.

The kingdom, therefore, was to go to another man. Saul was to lose it—but not at that moment. What the Lord said was advance warning of what was to come. Saul continued to rule, even though he had raised up a barrier against himself.

Regardless of Saul, the Lord still recognized the people as his own; he was not willing that the idolatrous Philistines should destroy them, nor would he make the people suffer for Saul's disobedience. The Twelve Tribes were still the Lord's charge.

Jonathan, the son of Saul, was a valiant warrior for Israel. When he saw the large Philistine army ready to attack and realized that his people were not mobilized for the battle, he determined on some private intrigue of his own.

As a ruse, he and his armor bearer went to an outpost of the Philistine army, pretending to be friendly. "And Jonathan said unto his armourbearer, Come up after me: for the Lord hath delivered them into the hand of Israel."

The two men attacked the guards at the outpost and killed them. Twenty Philistines fell in this attack. Then the Lord sent a sharp earthquake so "there was trembling in the host [of Philistines], in the field, and among all the people . . . and the earth quaked. . . . The multitude melted away, and they went on beating down one another. . . . behold, every man's sword was against his fellow, and there was a very great discomfiture."

Then "all the men of Israel which had hid themselves in mount Ephraim, when they heard that the Philistines fled, even they also followed hard after them in the battle. So the Lord saved Israel that day." (1 Samuel 14:1-23.)

Chapter Nine

JONATHAN IS SPARED

In some respects, Saul resembled the Medes and the Persians who refused to change any law regardless of the circumstances. His discipline was strict and harsh. His son Jonathan almost lost his life because of it.

When the Lord used an earthquake to break up the Philistine battle preparations at Michmash, the Hebrews came out of hiding and pursued the Philistines as they fled from the danger area.

All Israel took heart as they saw the turn of events, and Saul was jubilant. He ordered all his soldiers to press the pursuit all that day, and not stop even to eat. He "adjured the people, saying, Cursed be the man that eateth any food until evening, that I may be avenged on mine enemies. So none of the people tasted any food." It distressed the people, but all obeyed, for they feared Saul's revenge.

Some of the soldiers did not get word of Saul's command, including his own son Jonathan. As he was pursuing the Philistines through a forest, and being hungry, he saw a honeycomb that had fallen out of a tree. Not having heard of his father's charge, "he put forth the end of the rod that was in his hand, and dipped it in an honeycomb, and put his hand to his mouth; and his eyes were enlightened.

"Then answered one of the people, and said, Thy father straitly charged the people with an oath, saying, Cursed be the man that eateth any food this day. And the people were faint.

"Then said Jonathan, My father hath troubled the land: see, I pray you, how mine eyes have been enlightened, because I tasted a little of this honey. How much more, if haply the people had eaten freely to day of the spoil of their enemies which they found? for had there not been now a much greater slaughter among the Philistines?

"And they smote the Philistines that day from Michmash to

Aijalon: and the people were very faint. And the people flew upon the spoil, and took sheep, and oxen, and calves, and slew them on the ground: and the people did eat them with the blood.''

But Saul had decreed death to any who disobeyed his order. ''As the Lord liveth, which saveth Israel, though it be in Jonathan my son, he shall surely die. But there was not a man among all the people that answered him.''

An indication came to him that Jonathan had eaten, so Saul said to Jonathan: ''Tell me what thou hast done. And Jonathan told him, and said, I did but taste a little honey with the end of the rod that was in mine hand, and, lo, I must die. And Saul answered, God do so and more also: for thou shalt surely die, Jonathan.''

The people loved Jonathan and took his part. They said to Saul: ''Shall Jonathan die, who hath wrought this great salvation in Israel? God forbid: as the Lord liveth, there shall not one hair of his head fall to the ground; for he hath wrought with God this day. So the people rescued Jonathan, that he died not.''

They gave Jonathan credit for confusing the Philistines as he and his armor bearer attacked the outpost just before the great earthquake scattered the Philistines.

When Saul heard this he relented, and Jonathan was spared. (1 Samuel 14.)

Chapter Ten

"TO OBEY IS BETTER..."

The Lord's charge to Saul was to free Israel from the Philistines, and this the king endeavored to do. Although the Lord said he would take the throne from Saul's family because of continued disobedience, he nevertheless used Saul to carry on his fight with their implacable enemy.

"And there was sore war against the Philistines all the days of Saul: and when Saul saw any strong man, or any valiant man, he took him unto him."(1 Samuel 14:52.)

The Lord now gave Saul a particular assignment: destroy the people of Amalek! The Lord was ready to punish the Amalekites for their present corruption, but also for the attacks they made on Israel in the days of Moses as the tribes came up from Egypt.

It will be remembered that this was the occasion when Moses held his hands high above his head as Joshua led the Hebrews in battle. As long as Moses' hands were held high, Israel was victorious. When he tired and lowered his hands, the Amalekites drove them back. It was then that Aaron and Hur held up Moses' arms, "and his hands were steady until the going down of the sun. And Joshua discomfited Amalek and his people with the edge of the sword." (Exodus 17:8-16.)

Now the prophet Samuel spoke to Saul and commanded:

"The Lord sent me to anoint thee to be king over his people, over Israel: now therefore hearken thou unto the voice of the words of the Lord.

"Thus saith the Lord of hosts, I remember that which Amalek did to Israel, how he laid wait for him in the way, when he came up from Egypt. Now go and smite Amalek, and utterly destroy all that they have, and spare them not; but slay both man and woman, infant and suckling, ox and sheep, camel and ass.

"And Saul gathered the people together, and numbered them in Telaim, two hundred thousand footmen, and ten thousand men of Judah."

It was a mighty army that Saul took to destroy the Amalekites—210,000 men.

"And Saul smote the Amalekites from Havilah until thou
comest to Shur, that is over against Egypt. And he took Agag the
king of the Amalekites alive, and utterly destroyed all the people
with the edge of the sword.

"But Saul and the people spared Agag, and the best of the
sheep, and of the oxen, and of the fatlings, and the lambs, and all
that was good, and would not utterly destroy them: but every
thing that was vile and refuse, that they destroyed utterly."
(Samuel 15:1-9.)

Here again Saul pitted his own judgment against that of the
Lord, and disobeyed a specific commandment. These Amalekites were so wicked that the Lord wanted them wiped off the
face of the earth, even their offspring, their livestock—everything. They were to be like Sodom and Gomorrah, obliterated
from the earth.

It was not done. Saul failed. Angered by this disobedience,
the Lord sent Samuel again to upbraid the king. According to the
Joseph Smith Translation of the Bible, the Lord said to Samuel,
"I have set up Saul to be a king, and he repenteth not that he hath
sinned, for he is turned back from following me, and hath not
performed my commandments. And it grieved Samuel; and he
cried unto the Lord all night." (JST, 1 Samuel 15:11.)

Then, continuing the King James Version, we read: "When
Samuel rose early to meet Saul in the morning, it was told
Samuel, saying, Saul came to Carmel, and, behold, he set him up
a place, and is gone about, and passed on, and gone down to Gilgal.

"And Samuel came to Saul: and Saul said to him, Blessed be
thou of the Lord: I have performed the commandment of the
Lord.

"And Samuel said, What meaneth then this bleating of the
sheep in mine ears, and the lowing of the oxen which I hear?

"And Saul said, They have brought them from the Amalekites: for the people spared the best of the sheep and of the oxen,
to sacrifice unto the Lord thy God; and the rest we have utterly
destroyed.

"Then Samuel said unto Saul, Stay, and I will tell thee what the Lord hath said to me this night. And he said unto him, Say on.

"And Samuel said, When thou wast little in thine own sight, wast thou not made the head of the tribes of Israel, and the Lord anointed thee king over Israel? And the Lord sent thee on a journey, and said, Go and utterly destroy the sinners the Amalekites, and fight against them until they be consumed. Wherefore then didst thou not obey the voice of the Lord, but didst fly upon the spoil, and didst evil in the sight of the Lord?

"And Saul said unto Samuel, Yea, I have obeyed the voice of the Lord, and have gone the way which the Lord sent me, and have brought Agag the king of Amalek, and have utterly destroyed the Amalekites. But the people took of the spoil, sheep and oxen, the chief of the things which should have been utterly destroyed, to sacrifice unto the Lord thy God in Gilgal.

"And Samuel said, Hath the Lord as great delight in burnt offerings and sacrifices, as in obeying the voice of the Lord? Behold, to obey is better than sacrifice, and to hearken than the fat of rams. For rebellion is as the sin of witchcraft, and stubbornness is as iniquity and idolatry. Because thou hast rejected the word of the Lord, he hath also rejected thee from being king."

Saul tried to excuse his disobedience and said to Samuel: "I have sinned: for I have transgressed the commandment of the Lord, and thy words: because I feared the people, and obeyed their voice. Now therefore, I pray thee, pardon my sin, and turn again with me, that I may worship the Lord.

"And Samuel said unto Saul, I will not return with thee: for thou hast rejected the word of the Lord, and the Lord hath rejected thee from being king over Israel.

"And as Samuel turned about to go away, he laid hold upon the skirt of his mantle, and it rent.

"And Samuel said unto him, The Lord hath rent the kingdom of Israel from thee this day, and hath given it to a neighbour of thine, that is better than thou. And also the Strength of Israel will not lie nor repent: for he is not a man, that he should repent."

Recognizing his own sad plight, Saul said to the prophet: "I have sinned: yet honour me now, I pray thee, before the elders of my people, and before Israel, and turn again with me, that I may worship the Lord thy God. So Samuel turned again after Saul; and Saul worshipped the Lord."

To further rebuke Saul for his defiance of the Lord's command, Samuel now called for the Amalekite king, Agag, to be brought before him. He said to the captive king, who had been bitterly cruel in destroying innocent women and children: "As thy sword hath made women childless, so shall thy mother be childless among women." Then Samuel himself killed Agag with a sword. (KJV, 1 Samuel 15.)

A sad commentary is that "Samuel came no more to see Saul until the day of his death: nevertheless Samuel mourned for Saul: and the Lord rent the kingdom from Saul whom he had made king over Israel." (JST, 1 Samuel 15:35.)

Samuel stayed away from Saul from this time on, and shortly afterward the old prophet died. The Spirit of the Lord seems to have abandoned Saul also, for we read, "The Spirit of the Lord departed from Saul, and an evil spirit which was not of the Lord troubled him." (JST, 1 Samuel 16:14.) It was another form of punishment for his transgression.

This evil spirit did not depart from Saul during the remainder of his reign. His temper became intolerable, his jealousy unbounded. He was ready to commit murder on the slightest provocation, and at one time he hurled a javelin at his own son, Jonathan.

This was a far cry from the day when God gave Saul a new heart as he commenced his reign, when the spirit of God was his companion, and even when he was given the gift of prophecy.

Chapter Eleven

THE WITCH OF ENDOR

It came to pass in those days, that the Philistines gathered their armies together for warfare, to fight with Israel. . . . When Saul saw the host of the Philistines, he was afraid, and his heart greatly trembled.'' (1 Samuel 28:1.)

If Saul sought the Lord for advice in his predicament, ''the Lord answered him not, neither by dreams, nor by Urim, nor by prophets.''

''Samuel was dead, and all Israel had lamented him, and buried him in Ramah, even in his own city, And Saul had put away those that had familiar spirits, and the wizards, out of the land.''

Completely frustrated in the face of this new war with the Philistines, Saul felt the need of guidance from some greater source. Since the Lord would no longer speak to him, he was willing to violate his own laws and turn to the occult. Therefore, he said to his servants, ''Seek me a woman that hath a familiar spirit, that I may go to her, and inquire of her. And his servants said to him, Behold, there is a woman that hath a familiar spirit at Endor.

''And Saul disguised himself, and put on other raiment, and he went, and two men with him, and they came to the woman by night: and he said, I pray thee, divine unto me by the familiar spirit, and bring me him up, whom I shall name unto thee.

''And the woman said unto him, Behold, thou knowest what Saul hath done, how he hath cut off those that have familiar spirits, and the wizards, out of the land: wherefore then layest thou a snare for my life, to cause me to die?

''And Saul sware to her by the Lord, saying, As the Lord liveth, there shall no punishment happen to thee for this thing.

''Then said the woman, Whom shall I bring up unto thee? And he said, Bring me up Samuel.

"And when the woman saw Samuel, she cried with a loud voice: and the woman spake to Saul, saying, Why hast thou deceived me? for thou art Saul.

"And the king said unto her, Be not afraid: for what sawest thou? And the woman said unto Saul, I saw gods ascending out of the earth.

"And he said unto her, What form is he of? And she said, An old man cometh up; and he is covered with a mantle. And Saul perceived that it was Samuel, and he stooped with his face to the ground, and bowed himself."

Whether Samuel's spirit in fact was there has been the subject of much controversy. Could a witch call a prophet of God back from the dead?

The King James Bible continues with this:

"And Samuel said to Saul, Why hast thou disquieted me, to bring me up? And Saul answered, I am sore distressed; for the Philistines make war against me, and God is departed from me, and answereth me no more, neither by prophets, nor by dreams: therefore I have called thee, that thou mayest make known unto me what I shall do.

"Then said Samuel, Wherefore then dost thou ask of me, seeing the Lord is departed from thee, and is become thine enemy? And the Lord hath done to him, as he spake by me: for the Lord hath rent the kingdom out of thine hand, and given it to thy neighbour, even to David:

"Because thou obeyedst not the voice of the Lord, nor executedst his fierce wrath upon Amalek, therefore hath the Lord done this thing unto thee this day. Moreover the Lord will also deliver Israel with thee into the hand of the Philistines: and to morrow shalt thou and thy sons be with me: the Lord also shall deliver the host of Israel into the hand of the Philistines.

"Then Saul fell straightway all along the earth, and was sore afraid, because of the words of Samuel: and there was no strength in him; for he had eaten no bread all the day, nor all the night."

The woman came to Saul and saw that he was troubled. She said unto him, "Behold, thine handmaid hath obeyed thy voice, and I have put my life in my hand, and have hearkened unto thy words which thou spakest unto me. Now therefore, I pray thee, hearken thou also unto the voice of thine handmaid, and let me set a morsel of bread before thee; and eat, that thou mayest have strength, when thou goest on thy way.

"But he refused, and said, I will not eat. But his servants, together with the woman, compelled him; and he hearkened unto their voice. So he arose from the earth, and sat upon the bed.

"And the woman had a fat calf in the house; and she hasted, and killed it, and took flour, and kneaded it, and did bake unleavened bread thereof: And she brought it before Saul, and before his servants; and they did eat. Then they rose up, and went away that night." (1 Samuel 28:2-25.)

When the Prophet Joseph Smith corrected this portion of the Bible, as we read it in the Inspired Version, he left it like this:

"Then said the woman, The word of whom shall I bring up unto thee? And he said, Bring me up the word of Samuel.

"And when the woman saw the words of Samuel, she cried with a loud voice; and the woman spake to Saul, saying, Why hast thou deceived me? for thou art Saul.

"And the king said unto her, Be not afraid; for what sawest thou? And the woman said unto Saul, I saw the words of Samuel ascending out of the earth. And she said, I saw Samuel also.

"And he said unto her, What form is he of? and she said, I saw an old man coming up, covered with a mantle. And Saul perceived that it was Samuel, and he stooped, his face to the ground, and bowed himself.

"And these are the words of Samuel unto Saul, Why hast thou disquieted me, to bring me up? and Saul answered, I am sore distressed; for the Philistines make war against me, and God is departed from me, and answereth me no more, neither by prophets, nor by dreams; therefore I have called thee, that thou mayest make known unto me what I shall do.

"Then said Samuel, Wherefore then dost thou ask of me, seeing the Lord is departed from thee, and is become thine enemy? And the Lord hath done to him, as he spake by me: for the Lord hath rent the kingdom out of thine hand, and given it to thy neighbour, even to David:

"Because thou obeyedst not the voice of the Lord, nor executedst his fierce wrath upon Amalek, therefore hath the Lord done this thing unto thee this day. Moreover the Lord will also deliver Israel with thee unto the hand of the Philistines; and tomorrow shalt thou and thy sons be with me; the Lord also shall deliver the host of Israel into the hand of the Philistines.

"Then Saul fell straightway all along on the earth, and was sore afraid, because of the words of Samuel; and there was no strength in him; for he had eaten no bread all the day, nor all the night." (JST, 1 Samuel 28:11-20.)

The view of the Church regarding the witch of Endor is clearly stated by President Charles W. Penrose, counselor in the First Presidency to both President Joseph F. Smith and President Heber J. Grant, who wrote the following concerning the matter:

"There are differences of opinion as to the facts narrated in the Bible concerning the visit of Saul, King of Israel, to the Witch of Endor and her purported interview with the spirit of the departed Prophet Samuel.

"The popular view of this matter is that the witch, at the request of King Saul, 'brought up' the spirit of Samuel and that Saul conversed with him and learned from him the fate which awaited him in his coming battle with the Philistines. But the question arises, how could a witch, who under the law of Moses was not to be permitted to live, and with whom consultation was forbidden by the Lord, have power to bring forth at her bidding the spirit of a holy prophet?

"In answer to this query it has been suggested that the woman was not really a witch, but a prophetess who was in hiding. Why she was under the necessity of concealing her whereabouts is not made to appear. It has been alleged that the 'prophetess' theory has been held by persons supposed to understand the question thoroughly. Be that as it may, careful investigation of the history of the event will show that there has been great misunderstanding of the subject. . . .

"It is clear that the woman whom Saul visited was one of the class placed under ban, by the commandment of God, because they practiced divination with familiar spirits. Neither prophets nor prophetesses were then banished from the land or held in disrespect. It was only persons condemned by the Mosaic law who had to hide from the effects of its enforcement.

"Saul had tried every legitimate means to obtain supernatural guidance, but, as he had departed from the Lord, the Lord had departed from him. There was no answer from heaven to his inquiries; there was no word of the Lord by prophets; there was no communication through the Urim and Thummim; there was no manifestation by vision or by dream; there was no whispering of the divine spirit.

"In his desperation, Saul turned to the opposite power. In that he sinned. He knew that he was violating the law of the Lord. When he was serving God, he 'put away those that had familiar spirits and the wizards out of the land,' but when he fell into darkness he sought the ways of darkness and sealed his own doom. It is written:

" 'So Saul died for his transgression which he committed against the Lord, even against the word of the Lord, which he kept not, and also for asking counsel of one that had a familiar spirit, to inquire of it.' (1 Chronicles 10:13.)

"The law of God concerning these forbidden arts was given through the prophet Moses, and forms part of the Mosaic code. As for instance:

" 'Regard not them that have familiar spirits, neither seek after wizards, to be defiled by them: I am the Lord your God.' (Leviticus 19:31.)

" 'There shall not be found among you any one that maketh his son or his daughter to pass through the fire, or that useth divination, or an observer of times, or an enchanter, or a witch, Or a charmer, or a consulter with familiar spirits, or a wizard, or a necromancer. For all that do these things are an abomination unto the Lord: and because of these abominations the Lord thy God doth drive them out from before thee.' (Deuteronomy 18:10-12.)

"The Witch of Endor, then, instead of being a prophetess of the Lord, was a woman that practiced necromancy; that is, communication or pretended communication with the spirits of the dead; but she was led by a familiar spirit. In other words, she was a spiritual medium, similar to those modern professors of the art, who claim to be under the control of some departed notable, and through him or her to be able to communicate with the dead.

"It should be observed that in the seance with the king of Israel, Saul did not see Samuel or anybody but the medium or witch. She declared that she saw an old man coming up and that he was covered with a mantle. It was she who told Saul what Samuel was purported to have said. Saul 'perceived that it was

Samuel' through what the witch stated to him.

"The conversation that ensued between Samuel and Saul was conducted through the medium. All of this could have taken place entirely without the presence of the prophet Samuel. The woman, under the influence of her familiar spirit, could have given to Saul the message supposed to have come from Samuel, in the same way that messages from the dead are pretended to be given to the living by spiritual mediums of the latter days, who, as in the case under consideration, perform their work at night or under cover of darkness.

"It is beyond rational belief that such persons could at any period, in ancient or modern times, invoke the spirits of departed servants or handmaidens of the Lord. They are not at the beck and call of witches, wizards, diviners, or necromancers. Pitiable indeed would be the condition of spirits in paradise if they were under any such control. They would not be at rest, nor be able to enjoy that liberty from the troubles and labors of earthly life which is essential to their happiness, but be in a condition of bondage, subject to the will and whims of persons who know not God and whose lives and aims are of the earth, earthy.

"Nor is it in accordance with correct doctrine that a prophetess or prophet of the Lord could exercise the power to bring up or bring down the spirits of prophets and saints at will, to hold converse with them on earthly affairs. That is not one of the functions of a prophet or a prophetess. The idea that such things can be done at the behest of men or women in the flesh ought not to be entertained by any Latter-day Saint. The Lord has said:

" 'And when they shall say unto you, Seek unto them that have familiar spirits, and unto wizards that peep, and that mutter: should not a people seek unto their God? for the living to the dead? To the law and to the testimony: if they speak not according to this word, it is because there is no light in them.' (Isaiah 8:19-20.)

"It has been suggested that in this instance the Lord sent Samuel in the spirit to communicate with Saul, that he might know of his impending doom; but this view does not seem to harmonize with the statements of the case, made in the scripture which gives the particulars. If the Lord desired to impart this information to Saul, why did He not respond when Saul inquired of him through the legitimate channels of divine communication?

"Saul had tried them all and failed to obtain an answer. Why should the Lord ignore the means he himself established, and send Samuel, a prophet, to reveal himself to Saul through a forbidden source? Why should he employ one who had a familiar spirit for this purpose, a medium which he had positively condemned by his own law?

" 'But,' it is argued, 'the prediction uttered by the spirit which was manifested on that occasion was literally fulfilled. Israel was delivered into the hands of the Philistines, and Saul and his three sons and his armor bearer and the men of his staff were all slain. It was therefore a true prophecy.'

"Admitting that as perfectly correct, the position taken in this article is not in the least weakened. If the witches, wizards, necromancers and familiar spirits, placed under the ban of the law, did not sometimes foretell the truth there would have been no need to warn the people against consulting them.

"If the devil never told the truth he would not be able to deceive mankind by his falsehoods. The power of darkness would never prevail without the use of some light. A little truth mixed with plausible error is one of the means by which they lead mankind astray. There is nothing, then, in the history of the interview between Saul and the woman of Endor which, rationally or doctrinally, establishes the opinion that she was a prophetess of the Lord or that Samuel actually appeared on that occasion.

"There is no satisfactory evidence that the spirits of the departed communicate with mortals through spiritual mediums or any of the means commonly employed for that purpose. Evil spirits, no doubt, act as 'familiars' or as 'controls,' and either personate the spirits of the dead or reveal things supposed to be known only to them and their living friends, in order to lead away the credulous, but those who place themselves under the influence of those powers of darkness have no means by which they can compel the presence of the spirits of the just or induce disclosures from them to the living. They are above and beyond the art of such individuals, and the mediums themselves are frequently the dupes of evil spirits and are thus 'deceivers and being deceived.'

" 'My house is a house of order, saith the Lord, and not a

house of confusion.' When God has anything to reveal, it will come in the way, by the means and through the persons whom he has appointed. If the living desire to hear from the dead, they should seek to the Lord, and not to those who presume to rush in 'where angels fear to tread.'

"The earthly sphere and the sphere of departed spirits are distinct from each other, and a veil is wisely drawn between them. As the living are not, in their normal condition, able to see and converse with the dead, so, it is rational to believe, the inhabitants of the spiritual domain are, in their normal condition, shut out from intercourse with men in the flesh. By permission of the Lord, persons on either side of the veil may be manifest to those on the other, but this will certainly be by law and according to the order which God has established.

"By observing that law and refraining from association with persons and influences that know not God and obey not his gospel, the Latter-day Saints will save themselves from subtle deception and much sorrow, and will be more susceptible to the light and inspiration and revelations that proceed from the Eternal Father!" (*Improvement Era* 1 [1898]: 495-500.)

The Prophet Joseph Smith warned strongly against evil spirits, mediums, and persons who "peep and mutter." He spoke of various ones in his day who professed false visions and revelations, and who spoke in unknown but false tongues. He otherwise sought to protect the Saints from the influence of the devil. President Joseph F. Smith was outspoken on this subject also. Said he:

"After all the horrors, persecutions, and cruelties that have been brought about by the senseless belief in witchcraft, it seems strange in this age of enlightenment that men or women, especially those who have received the gospel, can be found anywhere who believe in such a pernicious superstition. The Bible and history alike conclusively brand this superstition as a child of evil. In ancient times, God required the Israelites to drive the Canaanites from their land, and witchcraft was one of the crimes which he laid at the door of the Canaanites, and for which they were adjudged unworthy of the land which they possessed.

"Witchcraft has not infrequently been the last resort of the evil doer. Men bereft of the Spirit of God, when the voice of the

Lord has ceased to warn them, have frequently resorted to witchcraft, in the endeavor to learn that which Heaven withheld; and
the people of God from very early days to the present have been
troubled with superstitious and evil-minded persons who have
resorted to divination and kindred devices for selfish purposes,
and scheming designs. In the middle ages it rested like a night-
mare upon all Christendom.

"Let it not be forgotten that the evil one has great power in
the earth, and that by every possible means he seeks to darken the
minds of men, and then offers them falsehood and deception in
the guise of truth. Satan is a skilful imitator, and as genuine gospel truth is given the world in ever-increasing abundance, so he
spreads the counterfeit coin of false doctrine. Beware of his
spurious currency, it will purchase for you nothing but disap-
pointment, misery and spiritual death. The 'father of lies' he has
been called, and such an adept has he become, through the ages
of practice in his nefarious work, that were it possible he would
deceive the very elect.

"Those who turn to soothsayers and wizards for their information are invariably weakening their faith. When men began to
forget the God of their fathers who had declared himself in Eden
and subsequently to the later patriarchs, they accepted the devil's
substitute and made for themselves gods of wood and stone. It
was thus that the abominations of idolatry had their origin.

"The gifts of the Spirit and the powers of the holy Priesthood
are of God, they are given for the blessing of the people, for their
encouragement, and for the strengthening of their faith. This
Satan knows full well, therefore he seeks by imitation-miracles
to blind and deceive the children of God. Remember what the
magicians of Egypt accomplished in their efforts to deceive
Pharaoh as to the divinity of the mission of Moses and Aaron.
John the Revelator saw in vision the miracle-working power of
the evil one. Note his words. 'And I beheld another beast coming
up out of the earth; * * * And he doeth great wonders, so that he
maketh fire come down from heaven on the earth in the sight of
men, And deceiveth them that dwell on the earth by the means of
those miracles,' etc. (Rev. 13:11-14.) Further, John saw three
unclean spirits whom he describes as 'the spirits of devils,
working miracles.' (Rev. 16:13-14.)

''That the power to work wonders may come from an evil source is declared by Christ in his prophecy regarding the great judgment: 'Many will say to me in that day, Lord, Lord, have we not prophesied in thy name? and in thy name have cast out devils? and in thy name done many wonderful works? And then will I profess unto them, I never knew you: depart from me, ye that work iniquity.' (Matt. 7:22-23.)

''The danger and power for evil in witchcraft is not so much in the witchcraft itself as in the foolish credulence that superstitious people give to the claims made in its behalf. It is outrageous to believe that the devil can hurt or injure an innocent man or woman, especially if they are members of the Church of Christ—without that man or woman has faith that he or she can be harmed by such an influence and by such means. If they entertain such an idea, then they are liable to succumb to their own superstitions. There is no power in witchcraft itself, only as it is believed in and accepted.'' (*Gospel Doctrine,* pp. 375-77.)

The fact remains that the prediction made through the witch of Endor came true, regardless of its origin.

Chapter Twelve

THE LAST BATTLE

Israel was powerless before this latest Philistine invasion. The enemy was well equipped with chariots "made of iron," heavy armor for the men, and skilled archers who could shoot accurately from a distance. The Hebrews fled before them, and many were slain.

The Philistines particularly sought out Saul and his sons Jonathan, Abinadab, and Malchishua. "The battle went sore against Saul," and the archers hit him, badly wounding him.

Saul was afraid of being captured in this condition. Being unable to defend himself, he asked his armor bearer to draw sword and kill him, "lest these uncircumcised come and thrust me through and abuse me."

The armor bearer refused, "for he was sore afraid." So Saul drew sword himself, and with hilt toward the ground and the blade aimed directly at himself, he fell upon it. When the armor bearer saw that Saul was dead, he committed suicide in the same way. The scripture says: "So Saul died, and his three sons, and his armourbearer, and all his men, that same day together." (1 Samuel 31:1-6.)

It was the custom of the victors to "strip" the dead, taking anything of value from the corpses. While doing so, the Philistines found Saul and his three sons lying dead at Gilboa. They cut off Saul's head, removed his armor, and fastened the body to the wall of Beth-shan where all could see it. The head was put in the pagan temple of Dagon. (1 Chronicles 10:10.) The king's armor was placed in the temple of Ashtaroth, their heathen goddess. Then they "sent into the land of the Philistines round about, to publish it in the house of their idols, and among the people. . . .

"And when the inhabitants of Jabesh-gilead heard of that which the Philistines had done to Saul; All the valiant men arose, and went all night, and took the body of Saul and the bodies of his sons from the wall of Beth-shan, and came to Jabesh, and burnt them there. And they took their bones, and buried them under a tree at Jabesh, and fasted seven days.'' (1 Samuel 31:9-13.)

Another account of Saul's death is found in the first chapter of 2 Samuel. It reads as follows:

"Now it came to pass after the death of Saul, when David was returned from the slaughter of the Amalekites, and David had abode two days in Ziklag;

"It came even to pass on the third day, that, behold, a man came out of the camp from Saul with his clothes rent, and earth upon his head: and so it was, when he came to David, that he fell to the earth, and did obeisance.

"And David said unto him, From whence comest thou? And he said unto him, Out of the camp of Israel am I escaped.

"And David said unto him, How went the matter? I pray thee, tell me. And he answered, That the people are fled from the battle, and many of the people also are fallen and dead; and Saul and Jonathan his son are dead also.

"And David said unto the young man that told him, How knowest thou that Saul and Jonathan his son be dead?

"And the young man that told him said, As I happened by chance upon mount Gilboa, behold, Saul leaned upon his spear; and, lo, the chariots and horsemen followed hard after him. And when he looked behind him, he saw me, and called unto me. And I answered, Here am I.

"And he said unto me, Who art thou? And I answered him, I am an Amalekite. He said unto me again, Stand, I pray thee, upon me, and slay me: for anguish is come upon me, because my life is yet whole in me.

"So I stood upon him, and slew him, because I was sure that he could not live after that he was fallen: and I took the crown that was upon his head, and the bracelet that was on his arm, and have brought them hither unto my lord.

"Then David took hold on his clothes, and rent them; and likewise all the men that were with him: And they mourned, and wept, and fasted until even, for Saul, and for Jonathan his son, and for the people of the Lord, and for the house of Israel; be-cause they were fallen by the sword.

"And David said unto the young man that told him, Whence

art thou? And he answered, I am the son of a stranger, an Amalekite.

"And David said unto him, How wast thou not afraid to
stretch forth thine hand to destroy the Lord's anointed?

"And David called one of the young men, and said, Go near,
and fall upon him. And he smote him that he died.

"And David said unto him, Thy blood be upon thy head; for
thy mouth hath testified against thee, saying, I have slain the
Lord's anointed. And David lamented with this lamentation over
Saul and over Jonathan his son." (2 Samuel 1:1-17.)

The cry of Israel at that time might well have been "long live
the king; the king is dead." It was about in the year 1005 B.C. that
this took place.

Saul had risen like a meteor in a clear sky. He plunged to the
depths in his setting. Had he kept the commandments of the
Lord, he might have been one of the great prophet-kings of all
time, but he reaped the harvest of his own planting. Indeed, the
saddest words of mouth or pen are simply these: "It might have
been."

The scripture gives this epitaph upon Saul's life:

"So Saul died for his transgression which he committed
against the Lord, even against the word of the Lord, which he
kept not, and also for asking counsel of one that had a familiar
spirit, to inquire of it;

"And inquired not of the Lord: therefore he slew him, and
turned the kingdom unto David the son of Jesse." (1 Chronicles
10:13-14.)

PART III
KING DAVID: FROM SHEPHERD TO KING

*"I would not stretch forth mine hand
against the Lord's anointed."*
(1 Samuel 26:23.)

Chapter Thirteen

DAVID OF BETHLEHEM

King David was one of the most remarkable men in world history. Few were as versatile as he, few as gifted.

He was a soldier, a statesman, a liberator, a poet, and a musician. He conquered all the enemies of Israel and set up a kingdom that later became the envy of the world under the rule of his son Solomon.

He took Israel from degradation and despair to a position of power and respect, all within a few years. He went from being an unknown shepherd to Saul's armor bearer, then ultimately to the throne. Few people have achieved as he did. Few ever could!

It was the Lord's rejection of Saul that opened the door for David's ascent to the throne. He was chosen as a mere youth, but at the pinnacle of his success he was almost beyond compare. Where was there another such as he?

He was loyal to his king to the last; never did he raise his hand against him, even though the king was cruel and selfish and murderous at times.

Even the prophet Samuel was afraid of King Saul. He feared his vicious temper and his disregard for human life. He knew that Saul would kill at the least provocation. Yet Samuel mourned for Saul. He had seen his brilliant beginning. He knew the Lord had blessed him with his holy Spirit at first, and had given him the gift of prophecy. He knew, too, that Saul had been the Lord's own choice to be king over Israel, and that he had great promise of success.

And yet Saul had allowed his ego, his insane jealousy, his murderous disposition to destroy what might have been a glorious reign as a prophet-king. For this Samuel mourned.

It was long before Saul's death that the Lord rejected him. Samuel had warned Israel that a king could bring the people down to near slavery, and when he saw it happen before his own eyes, he was weighted down with grief.

Then the Lord spoke to him and said, "How long wilt thou mourn for Saul, seeing I have rejected him from reigning over Israel? fill thine horn with oil, and go, I will send thee to Jesse the Bethlehemite: for I have provided me a king among his sons." Samuel expressed his fear as he replied, "How can I go? if Saul hear it, he will kill me." (1 Samuel 16:1-2.)

How the mighty Saul had fallen, that he would kill even Samuel, who had anointed him king!

The Lord persisted, however, and instructed Samuel to go to the home of Jesse of Bethlehem, "and thou shalt anoint unto me him whom I name unto thee." The Lord told him to offer a sacrifice there on the altar and invite Jesse to the sacrifice.

"And Samuel did that which the Lord spake, and came to Bethlehem. And the elders of the town trembled at his coming, and said, Comest thou peaceably?

"And he said, Peaceably: I am come to sacrifice unto the Lord: sanctify yourselves, and come with me to the sacrifice. And he sanctified Jesse and his sons, and called them to the sacrifice.

"And it came to pass, when they were come, that he looked on Eliab, and said, Surely the Lord's anointed is before him.

"But the Lord said unto Samuel, Look not on his countenance, or on the height of his stature; because I have refused him: for the Lord seeth not as man seeth; for man looketh on the outward appearance, but the Lord looketh on the heart.

"Then Jesse called Abinadab, and made him pass before Samuel. And he said, Neither hath the Lord chosen this.

"Then Jesse made Shammah to pass by. And he said, Neither hath the Lord chosen this.

"Again, Jesse made seven of his sons to pass before Samuel. And Samuel said unto Jesse, The Lord hath not chosen these."

Samuel then said to Jesse, "Are here all thy children? And he said, There remaineth yet the youngest, and, behold, he keepeth the sheep. And Samuel said unto Jesse, Send and fetch him: for we will not sit down till he come hither.

"And he sent, and brought him in. Now he was ruddy, and withal of a beautiful countenance, and goodly to look to. And the Lord said, Arise, anoint him: for this is he.

"Then Samuel took the horn of oil, and anointed him in the midst of his brethren: and the Spirit of the Lord came upon David from that day forward. So Samuel rose up, and went to Ramah." (1 Samuel 16:1-13.)

In those days Saul was troubled with an evil spirit, which was calmed by music. Saul's servants said to him: "Let our lord now command thy servants, which are before thee, to seek out a man, who is a cunning player on a harp; and it shall come to pass, when the evil spirit, which is not of God, is upon thee, that he shall play with his hand, and thou shalt be well.

"And Saul said unto his servants, Provide me now a man that can play well, and bring him to me.

"Then answered one of the servants, and said, Behold, I have seen a son of Jesse the Bethlehemite, that is cunning in playing, and a mighty valiant man, and a man of war, and prudent in matters, and a comely person, and the Lord is with him.

"Wherefore Saul sent messengers unto Jesse, and said, Send me David thy son, which is with the sheep.

"And Jesse took an ass laden with bread, and a bottle of wine, and a kid, and sent them by David his son unto Saul. And David came to Saul, and stood before him: and he loved him greatly; and he became his armourbearer.

"And Saul sent to Jesse, saying, Let David, I pray thee, stand before me; for he hath found favour in my sight.

"And it came to pass, when the evil spirit, which was not of God, was upon Saul, that David took a harp, and played with his hand; so Saul was refreshed, and was well, and the evil spirit departed from him." (JST, 1 Samuel 16:16-23.)

Although Saul was rejected by the Lord, and Samuel had so notified him, it appears that the king as yet knew nothing of David's selection to succeed him. Returning for a time from his duties as a musician in Saul's court, David was back with his sheep.

David's anointing as king was done quietly and in the rural area where he was a shepherd. Nothing was done at this time to actually seat him on the throne. Saul still wore the crown and continued to do so until his death. All through the intervening time David made no pretense toward taking over the government. He remained in waiting.

Chapter Fourteen

DAVID
AND GOLIATH

War broke out again. David's three older brothers were called into Saul's army and were fighting the Philistines.

One day Jesse, David's father, said to his young son, "Take now for thy brethren an ephah of this parched corn, and these ten loaves, and run to the camp to thy brethren; And carry these ten cheeses unto the captain of their thousand, and look how thy brethren fare, and take their pledge. . . .

"And David rose up early in the morning, and left the sheep with a keeper, and took, and went, as Jesse had commanded him; and he came to the trench, as the host was going forth to the fight, and shouted for the battle. For Israel and the Philistines had put the battle in array, army against army.

"And David left his carriage in the hand of the keeper of the carriage, and ran into the army, and came and saluted his brethren." (1 Samuel 17:17-18, 20-22.)

Among the Philistines was a giant named Goliath, who stood over ten feet high. His brothers also were giants. One was named Lahmi. "Jair slew Lahmi, the brother of Goliath the Gittite, whose spear staff was like a weaver's beam. [This beam was a horizontal cylindrical bar in a loom upon which warp or woven cloth was wound.]

"And yet again there was war at Gath, where was a man of great stature, whose fingers and toes were four and twenty, six on each hand, and six on each foot: and he also was the son of the giant. But when he defied Israel, Jonathan the son of Shimea David's brother slew him.

"These were born unto the giant in Gath; and they fell by the hand of David, and by the hand of his servants." (1 Chronicles 20:5-8.)

Another giant was killed in those days also. We read in 1 Chronicles:

"Benaiah the son of Jehoiada, the son of a valiant man of Kabzeel, who had done many acts; he slew two lionlike men of Moab: also he went down and slew a lion in a pit in a snowy day. And he slew an Egyptian, a man of great stature, five cubits high; and in the Egyptian's hand was a spear like a weaver's beam; and he went down to him with a staff, and plucked the spear out of the Egyptian's hand, and slew him with his own spear.

"These things did Benaiah the son of Jehoiada, and had the name among the three mighties. Behold, he was honourable among the thirty, but attained not to the first three: and David set him over his guard." (1 Chronicles 11:22-25.)

A cubit is about eighteen to twenty-one inches, according to *Smith's Bible Dictionary*. Goliath was six cubits and a span, or more than ten feet tall, and his brother, Lahmi, was about nine feet. Goliath was heavily armed. His helmet was brass and he wore a coat of mail and a "target of brass between his shoulders" to protect him against attack from the rear.

"And he stood and cried unto the armies of Israel, and said unto them, Why are ye come out to set your battle in array? am not I a Philistine, and ye servants to Saul? choose you a man for you, and let him come down to me. If he be able to fight with me, and to kill me, then will we be your servants: but if I prevail against him, and kill him, then shall ye be our servants, and serve us.

"And the Philistine said, I defy the armies of Israel this day; give me a man, that we may fight together." Goliath frightened the Israelites, and not one of them would accept his challenge.

On David's arrival with the supplies for his brothers, he heard of Goliath's taunts and wondered why none of Saul's men would go out to give him battle. His brothers chided him. Others asked, "Have ye seen this man that is come up? surely to defy Israel is he come up: and it shall be, that the man who killeth him, the king will enrich him with great riches, and will give him his daughter, and make his father's house free in Israel.

"And David spake to the men that stood by him, saying, What shall be done to the man that killeth this Philistine, and taketh away the reproach from Israel? for who is this uncircumcised Philistine, that he should defy the armies of the living God? . . .

"And Eliab his eldest brother heard when he spake unto the men; and Eliab's anger was kindled against David, and he said, Why camest thou down hither? and with whom hast thou left those few sheep in the wilderness? I know thy pride, and the naughtiness of thine heart; for thou art come down that thou mightest see the battle.''

When Saul heard of David's discussions with his brothers and other Israelite soldiers, the king sent for him. "David said to Saul, Let no man's heart fail because of him; thy servant will go and fight with this Philistine.

"And Saul said to David, Thou art not able to go against this Philistine to fight with him: for thou art but a youth, and he a man of war from his youth.

"And David said unto Saul, Thy servant kept his father's sheep, and there came a lion, and a bear, and took a lamb out of the flock: And I went out after him, and smote him, and delivered it out of his mouth: and when he arose against me, I caught him by his beard, and smote him, and slew him.

"Thy servant slew both the lion and the bear: and this uncircumcised Philistine shall be as one of them, seeing he hath defied the armies of the living God.

"David said moreover, The Lord that delivered me out of the paw of the lion, and out of the paw of the bear, he will deliver me out of the hand of this Philistine. And Saul said unto David, Go, and the Lord be with thee.''

Saul was willing for David to go, since no one else, including himself, would. The two men must have been about the same size, for the king put his own armor on David. "And David girded his sword upon his armour, and he assayed to go; for he had not proved it. And David said unto Saul, I cannot go with these; for I have not proved them. And David put them off him.''

So David went out as a shepherd with staff and sling. He chose five smooth stones from the brook "and put them in a shepherd's bag which he had, even in a scrip; and his sling was in his hand: and he drew near to the Philistine.

"And the Philistine came on and drew near unto David; and the man that bare the shield went before him. And when the Philistine looked about, and saw David, he disdained him: for he was but a youth, and ruddy, and of a fair countenance.

"And the Philistine said unto David, Am I a dog, that thou comest to me with staves? And the Philistine cursed David by his gods.

"And the Philistine said to David, Come to me, and I will give thy flesh unto the fowls of the air, and to the beasts of the field.

"Then said David to the Philistine, Thou comest to me with a sword, and with a spear, and with a shield: but I come to thee in the name of the Lord of hosts, the God of the armies of Israel, whom thou hast defied. This day will the Lord deliver thee into mine hand; and I will smite thee, and take thine head from thee; and I will give the carcases of the host of the Philistines this day unto the fowls of the air, and to the wild beasts of the earth; that all the earth may know that there is a God in Israel.

"And all this assembly shall know that the Lord saveth not with sword and spear: for the battle is the Lord's, and he will give you into our hands.

"And it came to pass, when the Philistine arose, and came and drew nigh to meet David, that David hasted, and ran toward the army to meet the Philistine. And David put his hand in his bag, and took thence a stone, and slang it, and smote the Philistine in his forehead, that the stone sunk into his forehead; and he fell upon his face to the earth.

"So David prevailed over the Philistine with a sling and with a stone, and smote the Philistine, and slew him; but there was no sword in the hand of David. Therefore David ran, and stood upon the Philistine, and took his sword, and drew it out of the sheath thereof, and slew him, and cut off his head therewith. And when the Philistines saw their champion was dead, they fled.

"And the men of Israel and of Judah arose, and shouted, and pursued the Philistines, until thou come to the valley, and to the gates of Ekron. And the wounded of the Philistines fell down by the way to Shaaraim, even unto Gath, and unto Ekron.

"And the children of Israel returned from chasing after the Philistines, and they spoiled their tents.

"And David took the head of the Philistine, and brought it to Jerusalem; but he put his armour in his tent.

"And when Saul saw David go forth against the Philistine, he said unto Abner, the captain of the host, Abner, whose son is this youth? And Abner said, As thy soul liveth, O king, I cannot tell.

"And the king said, Inquire thou whose son the stripling is.

"And as David returned from the slaughter of the Philistine, Abner took him, and brought him before Saul with the head of the Philistine in his hand.

"And Saul said to him, Whose son art thou, thou young man? And David answered, I am the son of thy servant Jesse the Bethlehemite." (1 Samuel 17.)

Seeing David's bravery, Saul's son Jonathan took an immediate liking to him, and "Jonathan loved him as his own soul." From this time a close and lasting friendship developed between the two young men.

"And Saul took him that day, and would let him go no more home to his father's house. Then Jonathan and David made a covenant, because he loved him as his own soul. And Jonathan stripped himself of the robe that was upon him, and gave it to David, and his garments, even to his sword, and to his bow, and to his girdle." (1 Samuel 18:1-4.)

Chapter Fifteen

SAUL BECOMES JEALOUS

Following his defeat of Goliath, David was fully accepted by King Saul, who "would let him go no more home to his father's house." (1 Samuel 18:2.)

David went wherever Saul sent him, and he "behaved himself wisely." Saul gave him command over a thousand soldiers, "and he was accepted in the sight of all the people, and also in the sight of Saul's servants."

But trouble was brewing. David was too popular for Saul's liking. "When David was returned from the slaughter of the Philistine, . . . women came out of all cities of Israel, singing and dancing, to meet King Saul, with tabrets, with joy, and with instruments of musick."

This should have pleased the king, and probably did until they began to sing about David and compare his accomplishments with those of Saul. "Saul hath slain his thousands," they sang, "and David his ten thousands."

This was like gall to Saul, who "was very wroth, and the saying displeased him; and he said, They have ascribed unto David ten thousands, and to me they have ascribed but thousands: and what can he have more but the kingdom? And Saul eyed David from that day and forward."

Whenever the evil spirit came upon Saul, or when his anger rose and cast him into temper tantrums, he was vicious. His jealousy of David was now so high that he was willing to kill him to preserve his own vanity.

One day as Saul sat upon his throne, David played his harp nearby to soothe the king's feelings. But anger and jealousy reached the explosive point with Saul, who looked upon David with deep hatred. He hurled a javelin at him, thinking, "I will smite David even to the wall with it."

But David, sensing the problem, was ever watchful, and

when Saul threw the javelin, David quickly jumped to one side and saved his life. "And Saul was afraid of David, because the Lord was with him, and was departed from Saul. Therefore Saul removed him from him."

David never retaliated, but continued to serve Saul acceptably, always avoiding any conflict with the king. "Wherefore when Saul saw that he behaved himself very wisely, he was afraid of him. But all Israel and Judah loved David."

Saul was cunning, and he now planned to place David in a position in battle where the Philistines would be sure to kill him. Having made him commander of a thousand men, Saul said to himself, "Let not mine hand be upon him, but let the hand of the Philistines be upon him." It was a murderous scheme.

As a ruse to give the appearance of friendliness and confidence, the king offered David the hand of his daughter Merab in marriage, saying at the same time, "Only be thou valiant for me, and fight the Lord's battles." He still had in mind putting David in hot combat where he would be killed.

Later on, David used the same tactics in his dealings with Uriah. After despoiling Uriah's wife, David deliberately schemed to place him in the midst of the battle where he would meet certain death. And there he died, for which the denunciation of Almighty God came upon the king.

David was not pleased with Saul's marriage proposal, and he said, "Who am I? and what is my life, or my father's family in Israel, that I should be son in law to the king?"

Apparently the marriage was arranged, but before it was solemnized the king gave Merab to another man, probably to embarrass David.

But unknown to the king, his younger daughter Michal had fallen in love with David, and when Saul learned of this he was pleased. He said, "I will give him her, that she may be a snare to him, and that the hand of the Philistines may be against him." Then he said to David, "Thou shalt this day be my son in law."

Apparently David was not too impressed with this proposal of marriage either, since it became necessary for Saul to tell his servants: "Commune with David secretly, and say, Behold, the king hath delight in thee, and all his servants love thee: now therefore be the king's son in law.

"And Saul's servants spake those words in the ears of David. And David said, Seemeth it to you a light thing to be a king's son in law, seeing that I am a poor man, and lightly esteemed?

"And the servants of Saul told him, saying, On this manner spake David.

"And Saul said, Thus shall ye say to David, The king desireth not any dowry, but an hundred foreskins of the Philistines, to be avenged of the king's enemies. But Saul thought to make David fall by the hand of the Philistines.

"And when his servants told David these words, it pleased David well to be the king's son in law: and the days were not expired.

"Wherefore David arose and went, he and his men, and slew of the Philistines two hundred men; and David brought their foreskins, and they gave them in full tale to the king, that he might be the king's son in law. And Saul gave him Michal his daughter to wife.

"And Saul saw and knew that the Lord was with David, and that Michal Saul's daughter loved him.

"And Saul was yet the more afraid of David; and Saul became David's enemy continually.

"Then the princes of the Philistines went forth: and it came to pass, after they went forth, that David behaved himself more wisely than all the servants of Saul; so that his name was much set by." (1 Samuel 18.)

The marriage was accomplished, but it had its problems despite the love Michal had for David. Her love turned to hate.

When war broke out again, David fought with the Philistines "and slew them with a great slaughter; and they fled from him."

But Saul never relented in his efforts to kill David. He sent messengers to David's house "to watch him, and to slay him in the morning: and Michal David's wife told him, saying, If thou save not thy life to night, to morrow thou shalt be slain.

"So Michal let David down through a window: and he went, and fled, and escaped. And Michal took an image, and laid it in the bed, and put a pillow of goats' hair for his bolster, and covered it with a cloth.

"And when Saul sent messengers to take David, she said, He is sick.

''And Saul sent the messengers again to see David, saying, Bring him up to me in the bed, that I may slay him. And when the messengers were come in, behold, there was an image in the bed, with a pillow of goats' hair for his bolster.

''And Saul said unto Michal, Why hast thou deceived me so, and sent away mine enemy, that he is escaped? And Michal answered Saul, He said unto me, Let me go; why should I kill thee?

''So David fled, and escaped, and came to Samuel to Ramah, and told him all that Saul had done to him. And he and Samuel went and dwelt in Naioth.'' (19:8-18.)

Since Michal's marriage to David no longer suited Saul's purpose, the king broke it off and gave Michal to another man. This infuriated David and widened the breach even more.

Chapter Sixteen

THE STRENGTH OF DAVID

David was a man "after God's own heart." In only one instance did he displease the Lord. Otherwise he did that which was right in the sight of God throughout his life.

So determined was he to serve the Lord in all he did that he constantly refused to retaliate when Saul attacked him. Always in his mind was one great principle: He would not lift his hand against the Lord's anointed.

What a lesson this is even for us today! He would not raise his hand or his voice against the Lord's anointed. He constantly served Saul in everything the king assigned him. He fought the king's enemies and won victory after victory, all to the glory of the king. But Saul still sought his life relentlessly.

Jonathan was David's loyal friend. He knew that Saul was a murderer at heart, and that the king's enmity toward David was in no way justified. Therefore, working against his own father, Jonathan endeavored to protect David.

One day David said to Jonathan, "Behold, to morrow is the new moon, and I should not fail to sit with the king at meat: but let me go, that I may hide myself in the field unto the third day at even.

"If thy father at all miss me, then say, David earnestly asked leave of me that he might run to Bethlehem his city: for there is a yearly sacrifice there for all the family. If he say thus, It is well; thy servant shall have peace: but if he be very wroth, then be sure that evil is determined by him."

Jonathan had a plan by which he could forewarn David. He said, "To morrow is the new moon: and thou shalt be missed, because thy seat will be empty.

"And when thou hast stayed three days, then thou shalt go down quickly, and come to the place where thou didst hide thyself when the business was in hand, and shalt remain by the stone

Ezel. And I will shoot three arrows on the side thereof, as though
I shot at a mark.

"And, behold, I will send a lad, saying, Go, find out the arrows. If I expressly say unto the lad, Behold, the arrows are on
this side of thee, take them; then come thou: for there is peace to
thee, and no hurt; as the Lord liveth. But if I say thus unto the
young man, Behold, the arrows are beyond thee; go thy way: for
the Lord hath sent thee away."

David therefore hid in the field, "and when the new moon
was come, the king sat him down to eat meat. And the king sat
upon his seat, as at other times, even upon a seat by the wall: and
Jonathan arose, and Abner sat by Saul's side, and David's place
was empty.

"Nevertheless Saul spake not any thing that day: for he
thought, something hath befallen him, he is not clean; surely he is
not clean."

The next day, which was the second day of the month,
David's place was again empty. "Saul said unto Jonathan his
son, Wherefore cometh not the son of Jesse to meat, neither yes-
terday, nor to day?

"And Jonathan answered Saul, David earnestly asked leave
of me to go to Bethlehem: And he said, Let me go, I pray thee; for
our family hath a sacrifice in the city; and my brother, he hath
commanded me to be there: and now, if I have found favour in
thine eyes, let me get away, I pray thee, and see my brethren.
Therefore he cometh not unto the king's table."

Saul became very angry at Jonathan and cried, "Thou son of
the perverse rebellious woman, do not I know that thou hast chosen the son of Jesse to thine own confusion, and unto the confusion of thy mother's nakedness? For as long as the son of Jesse
liveth upon the ground, thou shalt not be established, nor thy
kingdom. Wherefore now send and fetch him unto me, for he
shall surely die."

Jonathan answered Saul and said, "Wherefore shall he be
slain? what hath he done?

"And Saul cast a javelin at him to smite him: whereby
Jonathan knew that it was determined of his father to slay David.

"So Jonathan arose from the table in fierce anger, and did eat
no meat the second day of the month: for he was grieved for

David, because his father had done him shame.''

The next morning Jonathan went out to the field at the time agreed upon with David, taking a young boy with him. He said to the youth, ''Run, find out now the arrows which I shoot.'' And as the lad ran, Jonathan shot an arrow beyond him.

When the lad came to the place where the arrow had landed, Jonathan cried out, ''Is not the arrow beyond thee? . . . Make speed, haste, stay not.'' The lad hurriedly gathered up the arrows and brought them back to Jonathan. Then Jonathan gave him his bow and arrow, telling him, ''Go, carry them to the city.''

As soon as the youth was gone, David stood up from his hiding place, fell on his face on the ground, and bowed himself three times. Then he and Jonathan embraced, kissed one another, and wept.

''And Jonathan said to David, Go in peace, forasmuch as we have sworn both of us in the name of the Lord, saying, The Lord be between me and thee, and between my seed and thy seed for ever. And he arose and departed: and Jonathan went into the city.'' (1 Samuel 20.)

Chapter Seventeen

DAVID THE FUGITIVE

Saul's pursuit of David never slackened, making it necessary for David to go into hiding. One day he came to the home of Ahimelech, the priest, who gave him food and drink. David, unarmed, asked the priest if there were some weapon there that he could take.

"And the priest said, The sword of Goliath the Philistine, whom thou slewest in the valley of Elah, behold, it is here wrapped in a cloth behind the ephod: if thou wilt take that, take it: for there is no other save that here. And David said, There is none like that; give it me.

"And David arose, and fled that day for fear of Saul, and went to Achish the king of Gath." (1 Samuel 21:2-10.)

David found refuge in the cave of Addulam, "and when his brethren and all his father's house heard it, they went down thither to him."

Others also heard of David's hiding place, and "every one that was in debt, and every one that was discontented, gathered themselves unto him; and he became a captain over them: and there were with him about four hundred men."

Now David had the nucleus of a little army of his own. His father and mother were still with him in the cave. He feared for their safety, for Saul was without pity, so he took them to Moab and left them there for safekeeping while he took his small fighting force away.

The prophet Gad then found David and said to him, "Abide not in the hold [in hiding]; depart, and get thee into the land of Judah," which David did.

Hearing of David's departure, Saul called his own immediate servants about him and denounced them severely for not spying on David and reporting his movements.

Doeg, an Edomite who was supervisor of Saul's servants, replied, ''I saw the son of Jesse coming to Nob, to Ahimelech the son of Ahitub. And he inquired of the Lord for him, and gave him victuals, and gave him the sword of Goliath the Philistine.''

Saul was furious. He sent for the priest, whom he charged with conspiracy, and promptly condemned Ahimelech and his entire group of priests to die.

When Saul commanded his servants to ''fall upon'' the priests and kill them, none would obey. Then he turned to Doeg, who had made the report about David and the sword of Goliath, and said, ''Turn thou, and fall upon the priests. And Doeg the Edomite turned, and he fell upon the priests, and slew on that day fourscore and five persons that did wear a linen ephod.

''And Nob, the city of the priests, smote he with the edge of the sword, both men and women, children and sucklings, and oxen, and asses, and sheep, with the edge of the sword.

One of the sons of Ahimelech, a man named Abiathar, escaped and fled after David. ''And Abiathar shewed David that Saul had slain the Lord's priests.

''And David said unto Abiathar, I knew it that day, when Doeg the Edomite was there, that he would surely tell Saul: I have occasioned the death of all the persons of thy father's house. Abide thou with me, fear not: for he that seeketh my life seeketh thy life: but with me thou shalt be in safeguard.'' (1 Samuel 22.)

So far had Saul fallen! Human life meant little to him, and apparently he saw nothing sacred in the priesthood either.

Later, as Saul was returning from following the Philistines, he was told, ''Behold, David is in the wilderness of Engedi.'' So Saul took three thousand men and went out to find David and his men ''upon the rocks of the wild goats.''

Saul ''came to the sheepcotes by the way, where was a cave; and Saul went in to cover his feet: and David and his men remained in the sides of the cave.

''And the men of David said unto him, Behold the day of which the Lord said unto thee, Behold, I will deliver thine enemy into thine hand, that thou mayest do to him as it shall seem good unto thee. Then David arose, and cut off the skirt of Saul's robe privily.

''And it came to pass afterward, that David's heart smote him, because he had cut off Saul's skirt.

"And he said unto his men, The Lord forbid that I should do this thing unto my master, the Lord's anointed, to stretch forth mine hand against him, seeing he is the anointed of the Lord. So David stayed his servants with these words, and suffered them not to rise against Saul. But Saul rose up out of the cave, and went on his way."

Suddenly David ran out of the cave and cried after Saul, "My lord the king." When Saul turned to look at him, David bowed low before him and said, "Wherefore hearest thou men's words, saying, Behold, David seeketh thy hurt?

"Behold, this day thine eyes have seen how that the Lord had delivered thee to day into mine hand in the cave: and some bade me kill thee: but mine eye spared thee; and I said, I will not put forth mine hand against my lord; for he is the Lord's anointed.

"Moreover, my father, see, yea, see the skirt of thy robe in my hand: for in that I cut off the skirt of thy robe, and killed thee not, know thou and see that there is neither evil nor transgression in mine hand, and I have not sinned against thee; yet thou huntest my soul to take it.

"The Lord judge between me and thee, and the Lord avenge me of thee: but mine hand shall not be upon thee."

Saul was a hypocrite as well as a vicious man. When David called to him after this episode, the fearful but deceptive king said, "Is this thy voice, my son David? And Saul lifted up his voice, and wept.

"And he said to David, Thou art more righteous than I: for thou hast rewarded me good, whereas I have rewarded thee evil. And thou hast shewed this day how that thou hast dealt well with me: forasmuch as when the Lord had delivered me into thine hand, thou killedst me not.

"For if a man find his enemy, will he let him go well away? wherefore the Lord reward thee good for that thou hast done unto me this day.

"And now, behold, I know well that thou shalt surely be king, and that the kingdom of Israel shall be established in thine hand. Swear now therefore unto me by the Lord, that thou wilt not cut off my seed after me, and that thou wilt not destroy my name out of my father's house.

"And David sware unto Saul. And Saul went home; but

David and his men gat them up unto the hold.'' (1 Samuel 24.)

At another time also David spared the king's life. He and Abishai came upon Saul's camp at night and found the king there in a deep sleep.

"Then said Abishai to David, God hath delivered thine enemy into thine hand this day: now therefore let me smite him, I pray thee, with the spear even to the earth at once, and I will not smite him the second time.

"And David said to Abishai, Destroy him not: for who can stretch forth his hand against the Lord's anointed, and be guiltless? David said furthermore, As the Lord liveth, the Lord shall smite him; or his day shall come to die; or he shall descend into battle, and perish. The Lord forbid that I should stretch forth mine hand against the Lord's anointed: but, I pray thee, take thou now the spear that is at his bolster, and the cruse of water, and let us go.

"So David took the spear and the cruse of water from Saul's bolster; and they gat them away, and no man saw it, nor knew it, neither awaked: for they were all asleep; because a deep sleep from the Lord was fallen upon them.''

David then called from the top of a nearby hill and wakened both Saul and his chief guard, Abner.

"And David said to Abner, Art not thou a valiant man? and who is like to thee in Israel? wherefore then hast thou not kept thy lord the king? for there came one of the people in to destroy the king thy lord.

"This thing is not good that thou hast done. As the Lord liveth, ye are worthy to die, because ye have not kept your master, the Lord's anointed. And now see where the king's spear is, and the cruse of water that was at his bolster.

"And Saul knew David's voice, and said, Is this thy voice, my son David? And David said, It is my voice, my lord, O king.

"And he said, Wherefore doth my lord thus pursue after his servant? for what have I done? or what evil is in mine hand?''

Saul, the hypocrite, now replied again to David in the same deceitful tone as before: "I have sinned: return, my son David: for I will no more do thee harm, because my soul was precious in thine eyes this day: behold, I have played the fool, and have erred exceedingly.

"And David answered and said, Behold the king's spear! and let one of the young men come over and fetch it. The Lord render to every man his righteousness and his faithfulness: for the Lord delivered thee into my hand to day, but I would not stretch forth mine hand against the Lord's anointed. And, behold, as thy life was much set by this day in mine eyes, so let my life be much set by in the eyes of the Lord, and let him deliver me out of all tribulation.

"Then Saul said to David, Blessed be thou, my son David: thou shalt both do great things and also shalt still prevail. So David went on his way, and Saul returned to his place." (1 Samuel 26.)

Chapter Eighteen

SAUL'S LAST BATTLE

Time was running out for Saul. He had steadily lost battle after battle to the Philistines. He had alienated himself from the Lord and received no more help from him.

Samuel the prophet died, "and all the Israelites were gathered together, and lamented him, and buried him in his house at Ramah." David must have attended this funeral, for the record says that following it "David arose, and went down to the wilderness of Paran." (1 Samuel 25:1.)

Saul found himself in such straits, as the Philistines continued to press him and overrun his lands, that he felt the need of more than human guidance. His heart turned to Samuel. It was he who should be helping the king at this point, he felt—but Samuel was dead. That did not deter Saul. He would go to a spiritualist medium and have her bring back Samuel's spirit—as he thought.

Saul had driven the wizards and witches out of his kingdom. Knowing this, he nevertheless demanded of his servants that they find someone "who peeps and mutters" so that he could receive advice, if from no other source, then from the occult.

They found the witch of Endor, and after her seance, Saul felt worse than ever, convinced that his end was near. He fell "straightway all along on the earth, and was sore afraid, because of the words of Samuel: and there was no strength in him; for he had eaten no bread all the day, nor all the night.

"And the woman came unto Saul, and saw that he was sore troubled, and said unto him, Behold, thine handmaid hath obeyed thy voice, and I have put my life in my hand, and have hearkened unto thy words which thou spakest unto me. Now therefore, I pray thee, hearken thou also unto the voice of thine handmaid, and let me set a morsel of bread before thee; and eat, that thou mayest have strength, when thou goest on thy way.

"But he refused, and said, I will not eat. But his servants,

together with the woman, compelled him; and he hearkened unto
their voice. So he arose from the earth, and sat upon the bed.

"And the woman had a fat calf in the house; and she hasted,
and killed it, and took flour, and kneaded it, and did bake unleavened bread thereof: And she brought it before Saul, and before his servants; and they did eat. Then they rose up, and went
away that night." (1 Samuel 28.)

The king and his sons went out to battle, rallying their broken
forces the best they could. But in the fighting his sons were
killed. The "men of Israel . . . forsook the cities, and fled; and
the Philistines came and dwelt in them." (1 Samuel 31:7.)

Seeing he was defeated, Saul ignominiously took his own
life.

Chapter Nineteen

DAVID'S LAMENT

In this last battle David had not only seen Israel defeated and scattered, but he had also seen death come to the two men most prominent in his life—Saul, whom he still regarded as the Lord's anointed, and his bosom friend Jonathan. He grieved deeply.

"And David lamented with this lamentation over Saul and over Jonathan his son: . . .

"The beauty of Israel is slain upon thy high places: how are the mighty fallen!

"Tell it not in Gath, publish it not in the streets of Askelon; lest the daughters of Philistines rejoice, lest the daughters of the uncircumcised triumph.

"Ye mountains of Gilboa, let there be no dew, neither let there be rain, upon you, nor fields of offerings: for there the shield of the mighty is vilely cast away, the shield of Saul, as though he had not been anointed with oil.

"From the blood of the slain, from the fat of the mighty, the bow of Jonathan turned not back, and the sword of Saul returned not empty.

"Saul and Jonathan were lovely and pleasant in their lives, and in their death they were not divided: they were swifter than eagles, they were stronger than lions.

"Ye daughters of Israel, weep over Saul, who clothed you in scarlet, with other delights, who put on ornaments of gold upon your apparel.

"How are the mighty fallen in the midst of the battle! O Jonathan, thou was slain in thine high places.

"I am distressed for thee, my brother Jonathan: very pleasant hast thou been unto me: thy love to me was wonderful, passing the love of women.

"How are the mighty fallen, and the weapons of war perished!" (2 Samuel 1:17-27.)

This lament is considered to be one of David's superior literary compositions and ranks with the finest of his psalms.

David was exceedingly gifted in music and in poetry and skilled in combat. A wise organizer, he became the greatest governor of Israel since Moses. The measure of his talents and accomplishments can only be found in the fact that he was a man after God's own heart, and God magnified him.

Chapter Twenty

DAVID'S GREAT TASK

When Joshua led Israel into the Promised Land, he endeavored to conquer the strongholds of the Canaanites. The inhabitants, being extremely wicked, were destroyed by command of the Lord, as were their properties.

But some of the Canaanites were not defeated by Joshua. It was the plan of the Lord that they should remain as a thorn in Israel's side to afflict the tribes from time to time, humbling them and reminding them that God was their King and Deliverer.

The Lord said that even some of their idols would be left as a snare to the Hebrews, a test to see if true faith in the living God would survive among them.

But the Lord was now ready to move forward with his plans to make Israel a great nation as he had planned for it under Solomon. So David was given the responsibility of finishing what Joshua had left undone. The time had arrived when the Canaanites must be destroyed or "put under tribute."

With Solomon, the Lord would set up a kingdom that would reflect great credit upon His name that would then be honored by the heathen nations. They would see the great power, glory, and prosperity that God would shower upon the chosen tribes. So completion of the conquest must come now, and that was David's appointed task.

Following the death of Saul, David inquired of the Lord: "Shall I go up into any of the cities of Judah? And the Lord said unto him, Go up. And David said, Whither shall I go up? And he said, Unto Hebron." (2 Samuel 2:1.)

There was still great bitterness between Israel and Judah. The Twelve Tribes had not known harmony since the reign of the Judges when the unity built up by Joshua was lost, and when tribe fought tribe even over little things, with heavy loss of life.

David was of Bethlehem, so Judah accepted him as their

"favorite son." The men of Judah met him at Hebron, where the Lord had sent him, and there they anointed him their king.

To the north in Israel, Saul's former chief captain, Abner, took Ishbosheth, one of Saul's sons, and made him king over Ephraim and Benjamin "and over all Israel."

Ishbosheth was forty years old when he began his reign, but he wore the crown for only two years. Abner led a company of troops over to Gibeon, where they met some of David's men, and immediately a battle ensued. Abner and his men were beaten, and Abner fled for his life.

"And the children of Benjamin gathered themselves together after Abner, and became one troop, and stood on the top of an hill. Then Abner called to Joab, and said, Shall the sword devour for ever? knowest thou not that it will be bitterness in the latter end? how long shall it be then, ere thou bid the people return from following their brethren?

"And Joab said, As God liveth, unless thou hadst spoken, surely then in the morning the people had gone up every one from following his brother.

"So Joab blew a trumpet, and all the people stood still, and pursued after Israel no more, neither fought they any more. . . . But the servants of David had smitten of Benjamin, and of Abner's men, so that three hundred and threescore men died." (2 Samuel 2.)

Despite this truce, "there was long war between the house of Saul and the house of David: but David waxed stronger and stronger, and the house of Saul waxed weaker and weaker."

Abner and King Ishbosheth, Saul's son, quarreled over one of Saul's concubines. Abner was accused of infidelity, but he hotly rebuked the king, saying, "Am I a dog's head, which against Judah do shew kindness this day unto the house of Saul thy father, to his brethren, and to his friends, and have not delivered thee into the hand of David, that thou chargest me to day with a fault concerning this woman?

"So do God to Abner, and more also, except, as the Lord hath sworn to David, even so I do to him;

"To translate the kingdom from the house of Saul, and to set up the throne of David over Israel and over Judah, from Dan even to Beersheba.

"And he could not answer Abner a word again, because he feared him."

Abner now determined to communicate with David and to endeavor to turn the throne of Israel over to him. He sent messengers "to David on his behalf, saying, Whose is the land? saying also, Make thy league with me, and, behold, my hand shall be with thee, to bring about all Israel unto thee.

"And he said, Well; I will make a league with thee: but one thing I require of thee, that is, Thou shalt not see my face, except thou first bring Michal Saul's daughter, when thou comest to see my face.

"And David sent messengers to Ishbosheth Saul's son, saying, Deliver me my wife Michal, which I espoused to me for an hundred foreskins of the Philistines.

"And Ishbosheth sent, and took her from her husband, even from Phaltiel the son of Laish. And her husband went with her along weeping behind her to Bahurim. Then said Abner unto him, Go, return. And he returned."

Abner now talked with the elders of Israel and said, "Ye sought for David in times past to be king over you: Now then do it: for the Lord hath spoken of David, saying, By the hand of my servant David I will save my people Israel out of the hand of the Philistines, and out of the hand of all their enemies.

"And Abner also spake in the ears of Benjamin: and Abner went also to speak in the ears of David in Hebron all that seemed good to Israel, and that seemed good to the whole house of Benjamin.

"So Abner came to David to Hebron, and twenty men with him. And David made Abner and the men that were with him a feast.

"And Abner said unto David, I will arise and go, and will gather all Israel unto my lord the king, that they may make a league with thee, and that thou mayest reign over all that thine heart desireth. And David sent Abner away; and he went in peace."

But Joab, one of David's loyal men, was alarmed at Abner's visit, and said to David, "What hast thou done? behold, Abner came unto thee; why is it that thou hast sent him away, and he is quite gone? Thou knowest Abner the son of Ner, that he came to deceive thee, and to know thy going out and thy coming in, and to know all that thou doest.''

Then Joab, unbeknown to David, sent messengers after Abner and had him brought back from the well of Sirah.

When Abner returned to Hebron, Joab took him to one side ''and smote him there under the fifth rib, that he died.'' (2 Samuel 3:1-27.)

The death of Abner shocked King Ishbosheth, but ''his hands were feeble, and all the Israelites were troubled.'' While he lay sick in bed at noon, he was assassinated by two members of the tribe of Benjamin.

The assassins thought they were doing David a good service. They cut off the head of their victim and brought it to David, who was deeply offended and said, ''Shall I not therefore now require his blood of your hand, and take you away from the earth?

''And David commanded his young men, and they slew them and cut off their hands and their feet, and hanged them up over the pool in Hebron. But they took the head of Ishbosheth, and buried it in the sepulchre of Abner in Hebron.'' (2 Samuel 4.)

With the loss of both Abner and Saul's son, the northern tribes were without a leader. At last they were willing to consolidate with the south and accept David as king of all the tribes. A union of the entire Twelve Tribes was essential to the plans of the Lord, who now arranged to bring it about. With such an alliance, the Canaanites could be successfully controlled, and Israel could come into its intended glory under Solomon.

Chapter Twenty-one

THE UNITED KINGDOM

It was inevitable that the Twelve Tribes would come under one rule, and it was equally certain that David would be their king. Judah had accepted him. The time had come now when the other tribes were ready to do likewise.

During Saul's regime, David was a popular favorite. As the scripture says, "the people loved David." He had his enemies, of course, but the vast majority wanted him to be their ruler.

Beyond all that, however, was the decree of the Lord. It was he who had chosen David to be king, not only of Judah, but of all the Twelve Tribes. The Lord's plans required a united kingdom, not a divided one. The division had come because of the wickedness and the constant stubbornness of the people. Another division later on followed Solomon's reign for the same reasons.

With Saul's son now dead and his chief advocate, Abner, struck down by Joab, the elders and most of the people felt that the time had arrived to approach David and ask him to be their king.

"Then all Israel gathered themselves to David unto Hebron, saying, Behold, we are thy bone and thy flesh. And moreover in time past, even when Saul was king, thou wast he that leddest out and broughtest in Israel: and the Lord thy God said unto thee, Thou shalt feed my people Israel, and thou shalt be ruler over my people Israel.

"Therefore came all the elders of Israel to the king to Hebron; and David made a covenant with them in Hebron before the Lord; and they anointed David king over Israel, according to the word of the Lord by Samuel." (1 Chronicles 11:1-3.)

David was thirty years old when he became king, and he reigned for forty years. In Hebron he governed Judah alone for seven years and six months, and in Jerusalem he ruled thirty-three years over all Israel and Judah. (2 Samuel 5:1-5.)

By way of comparison with the King James Version of the Bible, we also give here passages from the *Holy Scriptures According to the Masoretic Text*. That version reads:

"Then came all the tribes of Israel to David unto Hebron, and spoke, saying, 'Behold, we are thy bone and thy flesh. In times past, when Saul was king over us, it was thou that didst lead out and bring in Israel; and the Lord said to thee: Thou shalt feed My people Israel, and thou shalt be prince over Israel.' So all the elders of Israel came to the king to Hebron; and king David made a covenant with them in Hebron before the Lord, and they anointed David king over Israel." (Philadelphia: Jewish Publication Society, 1955, p. 413.)

This was a most significant event. Not only did it end the long schism between the tribes, but it also laid the groundwork for the distinction God would give to Israel under Solomon, when a temple would be built there to the Most High and when the name of God would be held in respect and reverence even among the heathen nations.

It will be remembered that when the tribes were about to enter the Promised Land, after their long trek from Egypt, the Lord said he would make them the greatest nation on earth, if they would only serve him. When Moses was still with them, he addressed the tribes and said:

"This day the Lord thy God hath commanded thee to do these statutes and judgments: thou shalt therefore keep and do them with all thine heart, and with all thy soul.

"Thou hast avouched the Lord this day to be thy God, and to walk in his ways, and to keep his statutes, and his commandments, and his judgments, and to hearken unto his voice:

"And the Lord hath avouched thee this day to be his peculiar people, as he hath promised thee, and that thou shouldest keep all his commandments;

"And to make thee high above all nations which he hath made, in praise, and in name, and in honour; and that thou mayest be an holy people unto the Lord thy God, as he hath spoken." (Deuteronomy 26:16-19.)

In Deuteronomy 28, Moses reiterated this marvelous promise, saying:

'And it shall come to pass, if thou shalt hearken diligently unto the voice of the Lord thy God, to observe and to do all his commandments which I command thee this day, that the Lord thy God will set thee on high above all nations of the earth:

"And all these blessings shall come on thee, and overtake thee, if thou shalt hearken unto the voice of the Lord thy God."

Moses listed the blessings that would come to them, in their cities and in their fields, in their families and in their flocks, if they would serve God. He included this promise: "The Lord shall cause thine enemies that rise up against thee to be smitten before thy face: they shall come out against thee one way, and flee before thee seven ways." Then he added this important declaration:

"The Lord shall establish thee an holy people unto himself, as he hath sworn unto thee, if thou shalt keep the commandments of the Lord thy God, and walk in his ways.

"And all people of the earth shall see that thou art called by the name of the Lord; and they shall be afraid of thee.

"And the Lord shall make thee plenteous in goods, in the fruit of thy body, and in the fruit of thy cattle, and in the fruit of thy ground, in the land which the Lord sware unto thy fathers to give thee.

"The Lord shall open unto thee his good treasure, the heaven to give the rain unto thy land in his season, and to bless all the work of thine hand: and thou shalt lend unto many nations, and thou shalt not borrow." (Deuteronomy 28:1-12.)

All this promised success of course was subject to their becoming "an holy people unto himself." That was basic.

In David's day, through unification of the tribes and through their subsequent complete domination over the Canaanites, peace eventually came to the land. A fulfillment of this "greatest nation" prophecy now appeared to be possible. It was certainly approached under Solomon.

David was at Hebron when he was anointed king of Israel. Hebron was a small town in the hill country of Judah, twenty miles from Jerusalem, and was one of the most ancient cities in Palestine, known as far back as Abraham. (Genesis 13:18.) Isaac and Jacob lived there, as did Sarah. Joshua captured Hebron during the invasion. He assigned the city as a residence for the Levite priests and designated it as a city of refuge.

Hebron was the site of Absalom's ill-fated rebellion when he sought to take the kingdom away from his father, David. But David did not wish to make little Hebron his capital city for the united kingdom. He wanted Jerusalem for that purpose. However, that city was still held by the enemy and would yet have to be conquered. This David prepared to do.

Jerusalem was occupied then by the Jebusites, who were Canaanites, descended from the third son of Canaan. It was a heavily fortified city. On its outskirts was a citadel or castlelike fortress that the Jebusites thought to be impregnable. To stir up the spirit of combat among his men, David promised that the first man to destroy a Jebusite within that fortress would become one of the chief captains in his own army. With this incentive the battle began, and Joab was the first to claim a victim. In the attack both the castle and the city were taken.

For a time David stayed in the castle and called the fortress area the city of David, or the city of Zion. Subsequently the whole city was included in that designation.

There may be some confusion on this point, because Bethlehem, only five miles distant, was also known as the city of David, since the king grew up there and was anointed by Samuel on his father's farm nearby. Bethlehem was called so by the angelic herald announcing the birth of the Savior. The fact of the matter is that both cities—Bethlehem and Jerusalem—at different times were called the city of David.

The scripture now recounts: "And David went on, and grew great, and the Lord God of hosts was with him. . . . And David perceived that the Lord had established him king over Israel, and that he had exalted his kingdom for his people Israel's sake." (2 Samuel 5:10-12.)

Chapter Twenty-two

ANCIENT JERUSALEM

Jerusalem is believed to have been two thousand years old when David seized it. The name *Jerusalem* is first mentioned in the Bible in Joshua 10:1-27. Its king at that time was named Adonizedek, a name very similar to Melchizedek, who lived some five hundred years earlier in the time of Abraham.

Jerusalem has had several names. Because the Jebusites lived there in the time of David, the city also was known by Jebus. In Judges 19:10 we read "Jebus, which is Jerusalem."

The New Smith's Bible Dictionary says that the earliest name of the city was Urusalem, by which it was known before the Hebrew conquest of Palestine. It suggests that it was known by that name as early as the sixteenth century B.C. That would put it in the period of Melchizedek, who is definitely known in scripture as the king of Salem. Whether Salem was a short form of Urusalem may be left to the reader.

When David conquered the city, known then as Jebus, he changed the name back to Jerusalem, which could be a combination of Jebus and Urusalem, although the records are not clear.

The city had three principal hills, one of which was known as Zion; hence the frequent expression "Mount Zion." The elevation of the city is 2400 feet.

Smith's Bible Dictionary also says "Jerusalem was beseiged seventeen times; twice razed, its walls leveled." It was destroyed once by Titus the Roman general (A.D. 70), and in the days of Hadrian (A.D. 132) the temple site was plowed over and obliterated.

It is understood that the fortress David captured was located on the hill Zion, and for that reason David called his little area both Mount Zion and the city of David. However, later, the name was extended to the entire city of Jerusalem.

From Book of Mormon reading it will be recalled that during

the early part of the reign of Melchizedek, the city was desperately evil. Through his vigorous preaching under the power of the Lord, the people repented completely, and it became a model city. (Alma 13.)

The *Bible Companion*, edited by William Neal, says that the temple was erected on Zion, the highest of the three hills, and that Solomon's palace was nearby.

This volume suggests also that most of Solomon's wives, a thousand in all, lived in the citadel portion of town. He built a palatial home for his ''favorite wife'' near the palace on ''temple hill.'' The daughter of Pharaoh of Egypt, she lived for twenty-four years in the city of David.

It was in Jerusalem that Solomon erected the heathen shrines for idolatrous worship by his alien wives.

Chapter Twenty-three

BETHLEHEM OF JUDEA

What was so important about Bethlehem that both Jesus, the Prince of Peace, and David, Israel's greatest warrior, were born there?

Was there some eternal affinity between the Lord and David? Bethlehem was called the city of David. It was so announced by the angels who brought word to the shepherds telling of the Savior's birth.

Bethlehem, an ancient city, was already very old when David lived there. It is first mentioned in the Bible with reference to Rachel's death near Bethlehem. Both the later and the earlier names of the village are given. The text reads: "And Rachel died, and was buried in the way to Ephrath, which is Bethlehem." (Genesis 35:19.) It was there that Jacob set up a monument to her "that is the pillar of Rachel's grave unto this day."

The ancient name was generally known to the Hebrews as either Ephrath or Bethlehem-Ephrathah.

It was in the area of Bethlehem that Ruth met Boaz and that they raised their family. They were ancestors of both David and Christ.

There is no record of the actual origin of the village. It was a place of refuge for more than a century after the time of Ruth, but in the days of David it was threatened by King Saul, possibly because it was David's home and he hated David. David took Jesse and his family to Moab for safe-keeping during the wars then in progress.

Bethlehem was an outfitting place for travelers going to Egypt. Caravans were organized and equipped there. However, as Dr. William Smith says in his *Dictionary of the Bible*, "David did nothing to dignify or connect himself with it."

During the time of David, Bethlehem was fortified to serve as an armed gateway to Jerusalem. When Rehoboam, Solomon's son, was king, he maintained it for that purpose. It lost its population in the Babylonian captivity, but was repopulated when the Jews returned to Palestine.

Bethlehem is in that portion of Jordan which was occupied by Israel in the 1967 war. The area is very fertile. Its name means "house of bread" to the Jews. To the Muslims it meant "house of meat."

During the crusades, the Christians captured Bethlehem at about A.D. 1000, but later lost it to the Turkish Muslims. The Ottoman Turks gained control about A.D. 1500 and held it until World War 1. It was taken by British General Sir Edmund Allenby in 1917.

The Emperor Constantine caused to be built what has been called the Church of the Nativity, marking the supposed spot where Jesus was born. It was there that St. Jerome, a Catholic monk, translated the Bible from the Latin texts (5th century A.D.) and produced the Vulgate, which was the standard version of the Bible of the Roman Church for centuries.

Two Latin kings of Jerusalem were crowned in that old church, which later was demolished by Justinian, who then rebuilt it. Fragments of the murals dating back to the crusades still may be seen there. The site is now occupied by the Latin Church of St. Catherine.

Bethlehem has been a tourist center in recent years. It is said that as far back as the sixteenth century it was noted for its skilled craftsmen who did expert work in olivewood and mother-of-pearl. They still do a thriving tourist business. The actual population of the city is uncertain. Estimates range from 15,000 to 26,000. The ratio of Christians to Muslims is about sixty to forty.

One may speculate over the reason both David and Christ were born there. David certainly was a man after God's own heart. He must have been a powerful figure in the preexistent life, where Jehovah and he no doubt had much communication. It was a great compliment to David that Jesus chose his city as his birthplace.

On the other hand, the scripture indicates that Jesus descended below all things that he might rise above all things. He was born in a stable, presumably in one of the many limestone caves in the area.

Does this imply that Bethlehem was one of the lowliest places in Palestine, just as the stable was one of the lowliest of all places in which the Son of God might be born? Was this the reason the Lord chose Bethlehem as his birthplace?

Micah seems to suggest it: "But thou, Bethlehem Ephratah, though thou be little among the thousands of Judah. . . ." (Micah 5:2.)

Chapter Twenty-four

THE CONQUEST GOES ON

David's battles to conquer the Canaanites were no small engagements. Tremendous fighting forces were involved, and the casualties were very heavy.

At one time David is reported to have had an armed force of 1.3 million soldiers. (2 Samuel 24:9.) In another account he is credited with 1.5 million.

"And Joab gave the sum of the number of the people unto David. And all they of Israel were a thousand thousand and an hundred thousand men that drew sword: and Judah was four hundred threescore and ten thousand men that drew sword." (1 Chronicles 21:5.)

Men were killed on the battlefields by the tens of thousands. In just one such fight "the Syrians fled before Israel; and David slew the men of seven hundred chariots of the Syrians, and forty thousand horsemen." (2 Samuel 10:18.)

Such a loss seems colossal, and would be extremely high for battles fought by the armies of today. David's fighting was largely hand-to-hand combat, however, even where horsemen and chariots were involved. When it is realized that thousands of men stood in single hand-to-hand combat with other thousands, each man fighting to the death individually, it is understandable that there could be such great losses.

This makes more easily understood how such sudden and vast destruction of life could come at the Hill Cumorah in the final battle of the Nephites. Thousands fought singlehanded with other thousands there, each one seeking the life of the other, and at least one in each paired-off joust was killed. A single gladiator could slay many in a single day under these conditions.

Hence it is acknowledged to be quite possible for such heavy losses to occur in battles of this kind.

But not only were Israel's forces large. The forces of the

Philistines were large also. In one battle "the Philistines gathered themselves together to fight Israel, thirty thousand chariots, and six thousand horsemen, and people as the sand which is on the sea shore in multitude." (1 Samuel 13:5.)

What a fearsome sight it must have been to see thirty thousand chariots ready for battle, plus six thousand men mounted on horses, as well as numerous footmen. That battle force would strike fear in any opposing army.

When David smote Hadadezer "David took from him a thousand chariots, and seven hundred horsemen. . . . when the Syrians of Damascus came to succour Hadadezer king of Zobah, David slew of the Syrians two and twenty thousand men." (2 Samuel 8:4-5.)

When David challenged the Ammonites, they became so frightened that they sought aid from their neighbors. "The children of Ammon sent and hired the Syrians of Beth-rehob, and the Syrians of Zoba, twenty thousand footmen, and of King Maacah a thousand, and of Ishtob, twelve thousand." (2 Samuel 10:6.)

So mercenary soldiers are nothing new.

Following his victories, David put garrisons in Syria, Edom, Moab, and in various parts of the lands of the Philistines. The scripture says, "David reigned over all Israel; and David executed judgment and justice unto all his people." "And the Lord preserved David whithersoever he went." (2 Samuel 8:15, 14.)

An attempt had been made to bring the ark of God to the city of David. The king prepared to recover it with great pomp and ceremony.

"And they set the ark of God upon a new cart, and brought it out of the house of Abinadab that was in Gibeah: and Uzzah and Ahio, the sons of Abinadab, drave the new cart.

"And they brought it out of the house of Abinadab which was at Gibeah, accompanying the ark of God: and Ahio went before the ark.

"And David and all the house of Israel played before the Lord on all manner of instruments. . . .

"And when they came to Nachon's threshingfloor, Uzzah put forth his hand to the ark of God, and took hold of it; for the oxen shook it.

"And the anger of the Lord was kindled against Uzzah; and

God smote him there for his error; and there he died by the ark of God.

"And David was displeased, because the Lord had made a breach upon Uzzah: and he called the name of the place Perezuzzah to this day.

"And David was afraid of the Lord that day, and said, How shall the ark of the Lord come to me?

"So David would not remove the ark of the Lord unto him into the city of David: but David carried it aside into the house of Obed-edom the Gittite." (2 Samuel 6:3-10.)

When the ark had been there for three months, some of David's men told him that Obed-edom was highly prospered of the Lord because he had the ark. This gave David courage to try once more to bring it to Jerusalem. He made a place in which to house it and then prepared to move it.

"Then David said, None ought to carry the ark of God but the Levites: for them hath the Lord chosen to carry the ark of God, and to minister unto him for ever.

"And David gathered all Israel together to Jerusalem, to bring up the ark of the Lord unto his place, which he had prepared for it. And David assembled the children of Aaron, and the Levites." (1 Chronicles 15:2-4.)

David then addressed them and said: "Ye are the chief of the fathers of the Levites: sanctify yourselves, both ye and your brethren, that ye may bring up the ark of the Lord God of Israel unto the place that I have prepared for it.

"For because ye did it not at the first, the Lord our God made a breach upon us, for that we sought him not after the due order.

"So the priests and the Levites sanctified themselves to bring up the ark of the Lord God of Israel.

"And the children of the Levites bare the ark of God upon their shoulders with the staves thereon, as Moses commanded according to the word of the Lord.

"And David spake to the chief of the Levites to appoint their brethren to be the singers with instruments of musick, psalteries and harps and cymbals, sounding, by lifting up the voice with joy. . . .

"So David, and the elders of Israel, and the captains over thousands, went to bring up the ark of the covenant of the Lord out of the house of Obededom with joy.

"And it came to pass, when God helped the Levites that bare the ark of the covenant of the Lord, that they offered seven bullocks and seven rams.

"And David was clothed with a robe of fine linen, and all the Levites that bare the ark, and the singers, and Chenaniah the master of the song with the singers: David also had upon him an ephod of linen.

"Thus all Israel brought up the ark of the covenant of the Lord with shouting, and with sound of the cornet, and with trumpets, and with cymbals, making a noise with psalteries and harps." (1 Chronicles 15:12-16, 25-28.)

It was during this event that Saul's daughter, Michal, David's wife, turned against him. As she saw the king dance in the celebration, her love turned to hate and she despised him.

Chapter Twenty-five

DAVID'S KIND ACT

The close friendship of David and Jonathan was dear to the king. Although Jonathan was now dead, having been killed in Saul's last battle, David still felt an obligation to him. He said, "Is there yet any that is left of the house of Saul, that I may shew him kindness for Jonathan's sake?"

One of Saul's servants was a man named Ziba. He was summoned to come to David, who said to him, "Is there not yet any of the house of Saul, that I may shew the kindness of God unto him? And Ziba said unto the king, Jonathan hath yet a son, which is lame on his feet.

"And the king said unto him, Where is he? And Ziba said unto the king, Behold, he is in the house of Machir, the son of Ammiel, in Lodebar."

David sent for Mephibosheth, the son of Jonathan, and when the young man came to David, "he fell on his face, and did reverence. And David said, Mephibosheth. And he answered, Behold thy servant!"

David said to him, "Fear not: for I will surely shew thee kindness for Jonathan thy father's sake, and will restore thee all the land of Saul thy father; and thou shalt eat bread at my table continually.

Mephibosheth bowed before the king and said, "What is thy servant, that thou shouldest look upon such a dead dog as I am?"

David called to Ziba, Saul's servant, and said to him, "I have given unto thy master's son all that pertained to Saul and to all his house. Thou therefore, and thy sons, and thy servants, shall till the land for him, and thou shalt bring in the fruits, that thy master's son may have food to eat: but Mephibosheth thy master's son shall eat bread alway at my table."

Ziba had fifteen sons and twenty servants, and they all became servants of Mephibosheth.

"So Mephibosheth dwelt in Jerusalem: for he did eat continually at the king's table; and was lame on both his feet." (2 Samuel 9.)

Chapter Twenty-six

DAVID'S FIRST PSALM

The return of the ark of God was a great event in David's life and in the administration of Israel. After it was placed in its prepared place, "they offered burnt sacrifices and peace offerings before God.

"And when David had made an end of offering the burnt offerings and the peace offerings, he blessed the people in the name of the Lord.

"And he dealt to every one of Israel, both man and woman, to every one a loaf of bread, and a good piece of flesh, and a flagon of wine.

"And he appointed certain of the Levites to minister before the ark of the Lord, and to record, and to thank and praise the Lord God of Israel." (1 Chronicles 16:1-4.)

It was on this day that David "delivered first this psalm to thank the Lord." It reads:

"Give thanks unto the Lord, call upon his name, make known his deeds among the people.

"Sing unto him, sing psalms unto him, talk ye of all his wondrous works.

"Glory ye in his holy name: let the heart of them rejoice that seek the Lord.

"Seek the Lord and his strength, seek his face continually.

"Remember his marvellous works that he hath done, his wonders, and the judgments of his mouth;

"O ye seed of Israel his servant, ye children of Jacob, his chosen ones.

"He is the Lord our God; his judgments are in all the earth.

"Be ye mindful always of his covenant; the word which he commanded to a thousand generations;

"Even of the covenant which he made with Abraham, and of his oath unto Isaac;

"And hath confirmed the same to Jacob for a law, and to Israel for an everlasting covenant,

"Saying, Unto thee will I give the land of Canaan, the lot of your inheritance;

"When ye were but few, even a few, and strangers in it.

"And when they went from nation to nation, and from one kingdom to another people;

"He suffered no man to do them wrong: yea, he reproved kings for their sakes,

"Saying, Touch not mine anointed, and do my prophets no harm.

"Sing unto the Lord, all the earth; shew forth from day to day his salvation.

"Declare his glory among the heathen; his marvellous works among all nations.

"For great is the Lord, and greatly to be praised: he also is to be feared above all gods.

"For all the gods of the people are idols: but the Lord made the heavens.

"Glory and honour are in his presence; strength and gladness are in his place.

"Give unto the Lord, ye kindreds of the people, give unto the Lord glory and strength.

"Give unto the Lord the glory due unto his name: bring an offering, and come before him: worship the Lord in the beauty of holiness.

"Fear before him, all the earth: the world also shall be stable, that it be not moved.

"Let the heavens be glad, and let the earth rejoice: and let men say among the nations, The Lord reigneth.

"Let the sea roar, and the fulness thereof: let the fields rejoice, and all that is therein.

"Then shall the trees of the wood sing out at the presence of the Lord, because he cometh to judge the earth.

"O give thanks unto the Lord; for he is good; for his mercy endureth for ever.

"And say ye, Save us, O God of our salvation, and gather us together, and deliver us from the heathen, that we may give thanks to thy holy name, and glory in thy praise.

"Blessed be the Lord God of Israel for ever and ever. And all the people said, Amen, and praised the Lord." (1 Chronicles 16.)

Chapter Twenty-seven

DAVID'S DARKEST DAY

When the Lord spoke to the Prophet Joseph Smith about David, the Almighty said: ''In none of these things did he sin against me save in the case of Uriah and his wife; and, therefore he hath fallen from his exaltation, and received his portion.'' (D&C 132:38-39.)

David, the beloved of the Lord; David, the man after God's own heart; David, who offended the Lord in only one frightful instance, ''hath fallen from his exaltation, and received his portion.''

What a tragedy! Its extent is beyond our mortal comprehension. When we consider for a moment what exaltation means, that through it we may become like God himself, and then think of losing that mighty blessing, we come to some understanding of the necessity of obeying the laws of God in complete detail.

Throughout David's career the Lord helped and prospered him, and he was able to accomplish the mission to which he was assigned. He conquered the enemies of the people of God, completing the work originally started by Joshua. He extended the kingdom and became Israel's greatest warrior-king. He made ready for the building of the temple of the Lord. He wrote scores of inspiring psalms. ''And in none of these things did he sin.''

But then there was the case of Uriah and his wife. That made the whole tragic difference. That turned day into night, and reversed the king's ascent toward exaltation.

The Lord is just and he is merciful, but he does not allow mercy to rob justice. Where there is proper repentance, he forgives all but two sins: murder, wherein innocent blood is shed, and sin against the Holy Ghost. It was here that David's bark struck the deadly shoals. Even with David, beloved as he was, the Lord was no respecter of persons.

On Mount Sinai God proclaimed the moral code for Israel. It

included these three commandments:

Thou shalt not kill.

Thou shalt not commit adultery.

Thou shalt not covet thy neighbor's wife.

David violated all three. He knew the law well. He administered it for forty years. But for a fleeting moment he allowed lust to enter his heart, overcoming his better judgment. In yielding, he lost his place in the presence of the Lord even though he loved him so dearly.

The sad story is told in these few words:

"And it came to pass, after the year was expired, at the time when kings go forth to battle, that David sent Joab, and his servants with him, and all Israel; and they destroyed the children of Ammon, and besieged Rabbah. But David tarried still at Jerusalem.

"And it came to pass in an eveningtide, that David arose from off his bed, and walked upon the roof of the king's house: and from the roof he saw a woman washing herself; and the woman was very beautiful to look upon.

"And David sent and inquired after the woman. And one said, Is not this Bath-sheba, the daughter of Eliam, the wife of Uriah the Hittite?

"And David sent messengers, and took her; and she came in unto him, and he lay with her; for she was purified from her uncleanness: and she returned unto her house.

"And the woman conceived, and sent and told David, and said, I am with child.

"And David sent to Joab, saying, Send me Uriah the Hittite. And Joab sent Uriah to David.

"And when Uriah was come unto him, David demanded of him how Joab did, and how the people did, and how the war prospered.

"And David said to Uriah, Go down to thy house, and wash thy feet. And Uriah departed out of the king's house, and there followed him a mess of meat from the king.

"But Uriah slept at the door of the king's house with all the servants of his lord, and went not down to his house.

"And when they had told David, saying, Uriah went not down unto his house, David said unto Uriah, Camest thou not from thy journey? why then didst thou not go down unto thine house?

"And Uriah said unto David, The ark, and Israel, and Judah, abide in tents; and my lord Joab, and the servants of my lord, are encamped in the open fields; shall I then go into mine house, to eat and to drink, and to lie with my wife? as thou livest, and as thy soul liveth, I will not do this thing.

"And David said to Uriah, Tarry here to day also, and to morrow I will let thee depart. So Uriah abode in Jerusalem that day, and the morrow.

"And when David had called him, he did eat and drink before him; and he made him drunk: and at even he went out to lie on his bed with the servants of his lord, but went not down to his house.

"And it came to pass in the morning, that David wrote a letter to Joab, and sent it by the hand of Uriah.

"And he wrote in the letter, saying, Set ye Uriah in the forefront of the hottest battle, and retire ye from him, that he may be smitten, and die.

"And it came to pass, when Joab observed the city, that he assigned Uriah unto a place where he knew that valiant men were.

"And the men of the city went out, and fought with Joab: and there fell some of the people of the servants of David; and Uriah the Hittite died also.''

A messenger was sent to David with the account of Uriah's death. He reported: "And the shooters shot from off the wall upon thy servants; and some of the king's servants be dead, and thy servant Uriah the Hittite is dead also.

"Then David said unto the messenger, Thus shalt thou say unto Joab, Let not this thing displease thee, for the sword devoureth one as well as another: make thy battle more strong against the city, and overthrow it: and encourage thou him.

"And when the wife of Uriah heard that Uriah her husband was dead, she mourned for her husband.

"And when the mourning was past, David sent and fetched her to his house, and she became his wife, and bare him a son. But the thing that David had done displeased the Lord.'' (2 Samuel 11.)

The Lord sent the prophet Nathan to David immediately,

"and he came unto him, and said unto him, There were two men in one city; the one rich, and the other poor.

"The rich man had exceeding many flocks and herds: But the poor man had nothing, save one little ewe lamb, which he had bought and nourished up: and it grew up together with him, and with his children; it did eat of his own meat, and drank of his own cup, and lay in his bosom, and was unto him as a daughter.

"And there came a traveller unto the rich man, and he spared to take of his own flock and of his own herd, to dress for the wayfaring man that was come unto him; but took the poor man's lamb, and dressed it for the man that was come to him.

"And David's anger was greatly kindled against the man; and he said to Nathan, As the Lord liveth, the man that hath done this thing shall surely die: And he shall restore the lamb fourfold, because he did this thing, and because he had no pity.

"And Nathan said to David, Thou art the man. Thus saith the Lord God of Israel, I anointed thee king over Israel, and I delivered thee out of the hand of Saul;

"And I gave thee thy master's house, and thy master's wives into thy bosom, and gave thee the house of Israel and of Judah; and if that had been too little, I would moreover have given unto thee such and such things.

"Wherefore hast thou despised the commandment of the Lord, to do evil in his sight? thou hast killed Uriah the Hittite with the sword, and hast taken his wife to be thy wife, and hast slain him with the sword of the children of Ammon.

"Now therefore the sword shall never depart from thine house; because thou hast despised me, and hast taken the wife of Uriah the Hittite to be thy wife.

"Thus saith the Lord, Behold, I will raise up evil against thee out of thine own house, and I will take thy wives before thine eyes, and give them unto thy neighbour, and he shall lie with thy wives in the sight of this sun. For thou didst it secretly: but I will do this thing before all Israel, and before the sun.

"And David said unto Nathan, I have sinned against the Lord. And Nathan said unto David, The Lord also hath put away thy sin; thou shalt not die. Howbeit, because by this deed thou hast given great occasion to the enemies of the Lord to blaspheme, the child also that is born unto thee shall surely die.

"And Nathan departed unto his house. And the Lord struck the child that Uriah's wife bare unto David, and it was very sick.

"David therefore besought God for the child; and David fasted, and went in, and lay all night upon the earth. And the elders of his house arose, and went to him, to raise him up from the earth: but he would not, neither did he eat bread with them.

"And it came to pass on the seventh day, that the child died. And the servants of David feared to tell him that the child was dead: for they said, Behold, while the child was yet alive, we spake unto him, and he would not hearken unto our voice: how will he then vex himself, if we tell him that the child is dead?

"But when David saw that his servants whispered, David perceived that the child was dead: therefore David said unto his servants, Is the child dead? And they said, He is dead.

"Then David arose from the earth, and washed, and anointed himself, and changed his apparel, and came into the house of the Lord, and worshipped: then he came to his own house; and when he required, they set bread before him, and he did eat.

"Then said his servants unto him, What thing is this that thou hast done? thou didst fast and weep for the child, while it was alive; but when the child was dead, thou didst rise and eat bread.

"And he said, While the child was yet alive, I fasted and wept: for I said, Who can tell whether God will be gracious to me, that the child may live? But now he is dead, wherefore should I fast? can I bring him back again? I shall go to him, but he shall not return to me.

"And David comforted Bath-sheba his wife, and went in unto her, and lay with her: and she bare a son, and he called his name Solomon: and the Lord loved him." (2 Samuel 12:1-24.)

No matter what David's triumphs were, no matter the achievements of this mighty man in music, poetry, war or government, nothing could atone for his murderous act. Indeed, the saddest words of mouth or pen continue to be: "It might have been."

Chapter Twenty-eight

MORE TRAGEDY FOR DAVID

Family trouble mounted quickly and severely for David. New tragedy arose that cost the lives of two of his sons, one of whom murdered the other. It also blighted the life of one of his lovely daughters, described in scripture as being very fair.

The daughter, whose name was Tamar, was a full sister of Absalom, one of David's most aggressive sons.

By another wife David had a son named Amnon, who fell deeply in love with Tamar. He was lustful toward her, however, and tried to persuade her to sin with him. She steadily refused.

Amnon had a scheming cousin named Jonadab, "a very subtil man." Amnon said to him one day, "I love Tamar, my brother Absalom's sister.

"And Jonadab said unto him, Lay thee down on thy bed, and make thyself sick: and when thy father cometh to see thee, say unto him, I pray thee, let my sister Tamar come, and give me meat, and dress the meat in my sight, that I may see it, and eat it at her hand.

"So Amnon lay down, and made himself sick: and when the king was come to see him, Amnon said unto the king, I pray thee, let Tamar my sister come, and make me a couple of cakes in my sight, that I may eat at her hand."

David sent word to Tamar to go to her brother Amnon's house, "and dress him meat."

When Tamar arrived at Amnon's house, he was lying down. "And she took flour, and kneaded it, and made cakes in his sight, and did bake the cakes. And she took a pan, and poured them out before him; but he refused to eat. And Amnon said, Have out all men from me. And they went out every man from him."

Then Amnon said to Tamar, "Bring the meat into the chamber, that I may eat of thine hand." Tamar did as he requested, and "when she had brought them unto him to eat, he took hold of her, and said unto her, Come lie with me, my sister.''

She answered him, ''Nay, my brother, do not force me; for no such thing ought to be done in Israel: do not thou this folly. And I, whither shall I cause my shame to go? and as for thee, thou shalt be as one of the fools in Israel. Now therefore, I pray thee, speak unto the king; for he will not withhold me from thee.''

But Amnon would not hearken to her voice: ''being stronger than she, forced her, and lay with her.''

Then, the scripture says, ''Amnon hated her exceedingly; so that the hatred wherewith he hated her was greater than the love wherewith he had loved her. And Amnon said unto her, Arise, be gone.

''And she said unto him, There is no cause: this evil in sending me away is greater than the other that thou didst unto me. But he would not hearken unto her.

''Then he called his servant that ministered unto him, and said, Put now this woman out from me, and bolt the door after her.''

Tamar was wearing a garment of many colors, a costume traditionally worn by the king's daughters who were virgins. When the servant took her out of Amnon's chambers and bolted the door, she ''put ashes on her head, and rent her garment of divers colors.''

Absalom, her brother, found her in that condition and said, ''Hath Amnon thy brother been with thee? but hold now thy peace, my sister: he is thy brother; regard not this thing.'' So ''Tamar remained desolate in her brother Absalom's house.''

When King David heard what had happened, he was very angry.

''And Absalom spake unto his brother Amnon neither good nor bad: for Absalom hated Amnon, because he had forced his sister Tamar.''

Two years went by, with Absalom's anger burning deeply within him. He plotted to take the life of Amnon. An occasion arose when sons of David went out with the sheepshearers, and Absalom persuaded David to send Amnon along with them. He told his servants, ''Mark ye now when Amnon's heart is merry with wine, and when I say unto you, Smite Amnon; then kill him, fear not: have not I commanded you? be courageous, and be valiant.''

The servants did as Absalom had commanded; then all the king's sons arose, got on their mules, and fled.

''And it came to pass, while they were in the way, that tidings came to David, saying, Absalom hath slain all the king's sons, and there is not one of them left.

''Then the king arose, and tare his garments, and lay on the earth; and all his servants stood by with their clothes rent.''

But Jonadab, David's nephew and friend of Amnon, came to the king and said, ''Let not my lord suppose that they have slain all the young men the king's sons; for Amnon only is dead: for by the appointment of Absalom this hath been determined from the day that he forced his sister Tamar.

''Now therefore let not my lord the king take the thing to his heart, to think that all the king's sons are dead: for Amnon only is dead. But Absalom fled.''

When the king's sons returned to Jerusalem, they ''lifted up their voice and wept: and the king also and all his servants wept very sore. But Absalom fled. . . . And the soul of King David longed to go forth unto Absalom: for he was comforted concerning Amnon, seeing he was dead.'' (2 Samuel 13.)

But Absalom had none of the love for his father that David held for this rebellious son. He now plotted to dethrone his father and become king himself. One of David's saddest days came when he spoke of Absalom and said: ''Behold, my son, which came forth of my bowels, seeketh my life.'' (2 Samuel 16:11.)

Because his son had slain Amnon, David kept Absalom from the palace area under a tight prohibition. At last, however, through the persuasions of Joab, the king relented and told Joab, ''Go therefore, bring the young man Absalom again.''

Joab went to Geshur and brought Absalom back to Jerusalem. ''And the king said, Let him turn to his own house, and let him not see my face. So Absalom returned to his own house, and saw not the king's face.''

Absalom lived in Jerusalem for two years, but at no time was he allowed to see the king. Again Joab intervened and went to the king in the son's behalf. Finally David called for Absalom, who ''came to the king, and bowed himself on his face to the ground before the king: and the king kissed Absalom.''

Absalom now began to build up a secret force of followers loyal to himself, looking to the time when he would declare himself king. He was popular with the people and found it not difficult to recruit followers.

Absalom was handsome and ''in all Israel there was none to be so much praised as Absalom for his beauty: from the sole of his foot even to the crown of his head there was no blemish in him.

''And when he polled his head, (for it was at every year's end that he polled it: because the hair was heavy on him, therefore he polled it:) he weighed the hair of his head at two hundred shekels after the king's weight.'' (2 Samuel 14:21-26.) This vast amount of beautiful hair eventually proved to be the cause of his death, however.

Hypocritically, Absalom obtained permission of the king to go to Hebron, where David himself had been when he ruled Judah before becoming king of the united tribes. But Absalom was a liar and deceived his father. Said he, ''I pray thee, let me go and pay my vow, which I have vowed unto the Lord, in Hebron.

''For thy servant vowed a vow while I abode at Geshur in Syria, saying, If the Lord shall bring me again indeed to Jerusalem, then I will serve the Lord.

''And the king said unto him, Go in peace. So he arose, and went to Hebron.

''But Absalom sent spies throughout all the tribes of Israel, saying, As soon as ye hear the sound of the trumpet, then ye shall say, Absalom reigneth in Hebron.

''And with Absalom went two hundred men out of Jerusalem, that were called; and they went in their simplicity, and they knew not any thing.

''And Absalom sent for Ahithophel the Gilonite, David's counseller, from his city, even from Giloh, while he offered sacrifices. And the conspiracy was strong; for the people increased continually with Absalom.''

Word now came to David in Jerusalem that a general uprising had developed under Absalom, and ''the hearts of the men of Israel are after Absalom.

''And David said unto all his servants that were with him at

Jerusalem, Arise, and let us flee; for we shall not else escape from Absalom: make speed to depart, lest he overtake us suddenly, and bring evil upon us, and smite the city with the edge of the sword.'' (2 Samuel 15:7-14.)

With his servants and his family, the king fled and went into hiding. When Absalom and his men of war came to Jerusalem, they found the royal family gone.

David was not one to allow Absalom to take over the government in this way, much as he loved his son. He amassed his own army and prepared to fight it out. ''And David numbered the people that were with him, and set captains of thousands and captains of hundreds over them.''

The king's forces were under the command of Joab, who had served David well over the years. The king commanded Joab and his lieutenants, ''Deal gently for my sake with the young man, even with Absalom. And all the people heard when the king gave all the captains charge concerning Absalom.''

The battle went forward in the forests of Ephraim, an area heavily wooded, ''and there was there a great slaughter that day of twenty thousand men.

''For the battle was there scattered over the face of all the country: and the wood devoured more people that day than the sword devoured.

''And Absalom met the servants of David. And Absalom rode upon a mule, and the mule went under the thick boughs of a great oak, and his head caught hold of the oak, and he was taken up between the heaven and the earth; and the mule that was under him went away.

''And a certain man saw it, and told Joab, and said, Behold, I saw Absalom hanged in an oak.

''And Joab said unto the man that told him, And, behold, thou sawest him, and why didst thou not smite him there to the ground? and I would have given thee ten shekels of silver, and a girdle.

''And the man said unto Joab, Though I should receive a thousand shekels of silver in mine hand, yet would I not put forth mine hand against the king's son: for in our hearing the king charged thee and Abishai and Ittai, saying, Beware that none touch the young man Absalom.

"Otherwise I should have wrought falsehood against mine own life: for there is no matter hid from the king, and thou thyself wouldest have set thyself against me.

"Then said Joab, I may not tarry thus with thee. And he took three darts in his hand, and thrust them through the heart of Absalom, while he was yet alive in the midst of the oak.

"And ten young men that bare Joab's armour compassed about and smote Absalom, and slew him.

"And Joab blew the trumpet, and the people returned from pursuing after Israel: for Joab held back the people.

"And they took Absalom, and cast him into a great pit in the wood, and laid a very great heap of stones upon him: and all Israel fled every one to his tent."

In spite of this rebellion, the king never lost his love for Absalom. When he received word of his son's death he wept and cried out, "O my son Absalom, my son, my son Absalom! would God I had died for thee, O Absalom, my son, my son." (2 Samuel 18.)

Word was sent to Joab, telling him of the king's deep grief, "And the victory that day was turned into mourning unto all the people: for the people heard say that day how the king was grieved for his son.

"And the people gat them by stealth that day into the city, as people being ashamed steal away when they flee in battle.

"But the king covered his face, and the king cried with a loud voice, O my son Absalom, O Absalom, my son, my son!" (19:1-4.)

Thus ended Absalom's revolt.

Chapter Twenty-nine

THE TEMPLE IS PLANNED

As peace came to Israel and the enemy nations were conquered, David had an overpowering desire to build a temple to the Lord. The ark of the covenant had been kept always in a tent. No permanent house was provided for it. David desired to build one, but he was denied. Eventually when the temple was constructed, the ark found its permanent place there.

"Now it came to pass, as David sat in his house, that David said to Nathan the prophet, Lo, I dwell in an house of cedars, but the ark of the covenant of the Lord remaineth under curtains.

"Then Nathan said unto David, Do all that is in thine heart; for God is with thee.

"And it came to pass the same night, that the word of God came to Nathan, saying, Go and tell David my servant, Thus saith the Lord, Thou shalt not build me an house to dwell in: For I have not dwelt in an house since the day that I brought up Israel unto this day; but have gone from tent to tent, and from one tabernacle to another.

"Wheresoever I have walked with all Israel, spake I a word to any of the judges of Israel, whom I commanded to feed my people, saying, Why have ye not built me an house of cedars?

"Now therefore thus shalt thou say unto my servant David, Thus saith the Lord of hosts, I took thee from the sheepcote, even from following the sheep, that thou shouldest be ruler over my people Israel:

"And I have been with thee whithersoever thou hast walked, and have cut off all thine enemies from before thee, and have made thee a name like the name of the great men that are in the earth.

"Also I will ordain a place for my people Israel, and will plant them, and they shall dwell in their place, and shall be moved no more; neither shall the children of wickedness waste them any more, as at the beginning, And since the time that I commanded judges to be over my people Israel. Moreover I will subdue all thine enemies. Furthermore I tell thee that the Lord will build thee an house.

"And it shall come to pass, when thy days be expired that thou must go to be with thy fathers, that I will raise up thy seed after thee, which shall be of thy sons; and I will establish his kingdom.

"He shall build me an house, and I will stablish his throne for ever.

"I will be his father, and he shall be my son: and I will not take my mercy away from him, as I took it from him that was before thee: But I will settle him in mine house and in my kingdom for ever: and his throne shall be established for evermore.

"According to all these words, and according to all this vision, so did Nathan speak unto David." (1 Chronicles 17:1-15.)

David was a man of war—literally, it was said, "a man of blood." The Lord would not allow him to build the temple for that reason. But Solomon, David's son, was selected of the Lord to be the temple builder. He was a man of peace. The scripture says that the Lord loved Solomon.

But although he was not chosen to actually build the temple, David made many preparations for its construction:

"And David commanded to gather together the strangers that were in the land of Israel; and he set masons to hew wrought stones to build the house of God.

"And David prepared iron in abundance for the nails for the doors of the gates, and for the joinings; and brass in abundance without weight; Also cedar trees in abundance: for the Zidonians and they of Tyre brought much cedar wood to David.

"And David said, Solomon my son is young and tender, and the house that is to be builded for the Lord must be exceeding magnifical, of fame and of glory throughout all countries: I will therefore now make preparation for it. So David prepared abundantly before his death.

"Then he called for Solomon his son, and charged him to build an house for the Lord God of Israel.

"And David said to Solomon, My son, as for me, it was in my mind to build an house unto the name of the Lord my God:

"But the word of the Lord came to me, saying, Thou hast shed blood abundantly, and hast made great wars: thou shalt not build an house unto my name, because thou hast shed much blood upon the earth in my sight.

"Behold, a son shall be born to thee, who shall be a man of rest; and I will give him rest from all his enemies round about: for his name shall be Solomon, and I will give peace and quietness unto Israel in his days.

"He shall build an house for my name; and he shall be my son, and I will be his father; and I will establish the throne of his kingdom over Israel for ever.

"Now, my son, the Lord be with thee; and prosper thou, and build the house of the Lord thy God, as he hath said to thee.

"Only the Lord give thee wisdom and understanding, and give thee charge concerning Israel, that thou mayest keep the law of the Lord thy God.

"Then shalt thou prosper, if thou takest heed to fulfil the statutes and judgments which the Lord charged Moses with concerning Israel: be strong, and of good courage; dread not, nor be dismayed.

"Now, behold, in my trouble I have prepared for the house of the Lord an hundred thousand talents of gold, and a thousand thousand talents of silver; and of brass and iron without weight; for it is in abundance: timber also and stone have I prepared; and thou mayest add thereto.

"Moreover there are workmen with thee in abundance, hewers and workers of stone and timber, and all manner of cunning men for every manner of work.

"Of the gold, the silver, and the brass, and the iron, there is no number. Arise therefore, and be doing, and the Lord be with thee.

"David also commanded all the princes of Israel to help Solomon his son, saying,

"Is not the Lord your God with you? and hath he not given you rest on every side? for he hath given the inhabitants of the land into mine hand; and the land is subdued before the Lord, and before his people.

''Now set your heart and your soul to seek the Lord your God; arise therefore, and build ye the sanctuary of the Lord God, to bring the ark of the covenant of the Lord, and the holy vessels of God, into the house that is to be built to the name of the Lord.'' (1 Chronicles 22:2-19.)

Chapter Thirty

SOLOMON IS MADE KING

When David was "old and full of days, he made Solomon his son king over Israel." (1 Chronicles 23:1.)

"And David assembled all the princes of Israel, the princes of the tribes, and the captains of the companies that ministered to the king by course, and the captains over the thousands, and captains over the hundreds, and the stewards over all the substance and possession of the king, and of his sons, with the officers, and with the mighty men, and with all the valiant men, unto Jerusalem."

When these men were assembled, David stood before them and told them what the Lord had told him. "As for me," he said, "I had in mine heart to build an house of rest for the ark of the covenant of the Lord, and for the footstool of our God, and had made ready for the building:

"But God said unto me, Thou shalt not build an house for my name, because thou hast been a man of war, and hast shed blood.

"Howbeit the Lord God of Israel chose me before all the house of my father to be king over Israel for ever: for he hath chosen Judah to be the ruler; and of the house of Judah, the house of my father; and among the sons of my father he liked me to make me king over all Israel:

"And of all my sons, (for the Lord hath given me many sons,) he hath chosen Solomon my son to sit upon the throne of the kingdom of the Lord over Israel.

"And he said unto me, Solomon thy son, he shall build my house and my courts: for I have chosen him to be my son, and I will be his father.

"Moreover I will establish his kingdom for ever, if he be constant to do my commandments and my judgments, as at this day.

"Now therefore in the sight of all Israel the congregation of the Lord, and in the audience of our God, keep and seek for all the commandments of the Lord your God: that ye may possess this good land, and leave it for an inheritance for your children after you for ever."

The promise that Israel might "keep the good land" reminds us of the predictions of Moses as he prepared Israel to enter Palestine. The Lord was willing to bless his people with a great inheritance if only they would do their part. The blessings had to be earned.

David then turned to his son Solomon and said:

"And thou, Solomon my son, know thou the God of thy father, and serve him with a perfect heart and with a willing mind: for the Lord searcheth all hearts, and understandeth all the imaginations of the thoughts: if thou seek him, he will be found of thee; but if thou forsake him, he will cast thee off for ever. Take heed now; for the Lord hath chosen thee to build an house for the sanctuary: be strong, and do it."

It seems that the primary reason for Solomon's selection was to build the temple, thus providing the sanctuary for the ark of the covenant. That was a great objective of his administration.

David said further to Solomon: "Be strong and of good courage, and do it: fear not, nor be dismayed: for the Lord God, even my God, will be with thee; he will not fail thee, nor forsake thee, until thou hast finished all the work for the service of the house of the Lord." (1 Chronicles 28.)

David directed that Zadock the priest and Nathan the prophet should anoint Solomon king of both Judah and Israel, and this was done. "And they blew the trumpet; and all the people said, God save king Solomon.

"And all the people came up after him, and the people piped with pipes, and rejoiced with great joy, so that the earth rent with the sound of them." (1 Kings 1:39-40.)

Chapter Thirty-one

DAVID'S PREPARATIONS

Following the coronation, David "gave to Solomon his son the pattern of the porch, and of the houses thereof, and of the treasuries thereof, and of the upper chambers thereof, and of the inner parlours thereof, and of the place of the mercy seat.

"And the pattern of all that he had by the spirit, of the courts of the house of the Lord, and of all the chambers round about, of the treasuries of the house of God, and of the treasuries of the dedicated things:

"Also for the courses of the priests and the Levites, and for all the work of the service of the house of the Lord, and for all the vessels of service in the house of the Lord."

In addition, "he gave of gold by weight for things of gold, for all instruments of all manner of service; silver also for all instruments of silver by weight, for all instruments of every kind of service. . . .

"All this, said David, the Lord made me understand in writing by his hand upon me, even all the works of this pattern." (1 Chronicles 28:11-19.)

Then, addressing the kingdom, David said: "Solomon my son, whom alone God hath chosen, is yet young and tender, and the work is great: for the palace is not for man, but for the Lord God.

"Now I have prepared with all my might for the house of my God the gold for things to be made of gold, and the silver for things of silver, and the brass for things of brass, the iron for things of iron, and wood for things of wood; onyx stones, and stones to be set, glistering stones, and of divers colours, and all manner of precious stones, and marble stones in abundance.

"Moreover, because I have set my affection to the house of my God, I have of mine own proper good, of gold and silver, which I have given to the house of my God, over and above all that I have prepared for the holy house. . . .

"And who then is willing to consecrate his service this day unto the Lord?

"Then the chief of the fathers and princes of the tribes of Israel, and the captains of thousands and of hundreds, with the rulers of the king's work, offered willingly,

"And gave for the service of the house of God of gold five thousand talents and ten thousand drams, and of silver ten thousand talents, and of brass eighteen thousand talents, and one hundred thousand talents of iron.

"And they with whom precious stones were found gave them to the treasure of the house of the Lord. . . .

"Then the people rejoiced, for that they offered willingly, because with perfect heart they offered willingly to the Lord: and David the king also rejoiced with great joy."

Like a prophet inspired abundantly by the Lord, David then offered this prayer:

"Blessed be thou, Lord God of Israel our father, for ever and ever.

"Thine, O Lord, is the greatness, and the power, and the glory, and the victory, and the majesty: for all that is in the heaven and in the earth is thine; thine is the kingdom, O Lord, and thou art exalted as head above all.

"Both riches and honour come of thee, and thou reignest over all; and in thine hand is power and might; and in thine hand it is to make great, and to give strength unto all.

"Now therefore, our God, we thank thee, and praise thy glorious name.

"But who am I, and what is my people, that we should be able to offer so willingly after this sort? for all things come of thee, and of thine own have we given thee.

"For we are strangers before thee, and sojourners, as were all our fathers: our days on the earth are as a shadow, and there is none abiding.

"O Lord our God, all this store that we have prepared to build thee an house for thine holy name cometh of thine hand, and is all thine own.

"I know also, my God, that thou triest the heart, and hast pleasure in uprightness. As for me, in the uprightness of mine heart I have willingly offered all these things: and now have I seen with joy thy people, which are present here, to offer willingly unto thee.

"O Lord God of Abraham, Isaac, and of Israel, our fathers, keep this for ever in the imagination of the thoughts of the heart of thy people, and prepare their heart unto thee."

David continued his plea to the Lord, again in behalf of his son who was selected for this great responsibility. He prayed: "And give unto Solomon my son a perfect heart, to keep thy commandments, thy testimonies, and thy statutes, and to do all these things, and to build the palace, for the which I have made provision."

David then turned to the congregation and said: "Now bless the Lord your God."

The congregation bowed their heads and worshipped the Lord, blessing and thanking him for all his kindness.

"And they sacrificed sacrifices unto the Lord, and offered burnt offerings unto the Lord, on the morrow after that day, even a thousand bullocks, a thousand rams, and a thousand lambs, with their drink offerings, and sacrifices in abundance for all Israel:

"And did eat and drink before the Lord on that day with great gladness. And they made Solomon the son of David king the second time, and anointed him unto the Lord to be the chief governor, and Zadok to be priest." (1 Chronicles 29.)

Chapter Thirty-two

SOLOMON IS THREATENED

Beautiful as was the coronation of Solomon, and blessed as he was with the Spirit of the Lord, and having full support of the congregation of Israel, a threat was raised against his reign.

One of David's other sons plotted against him and determined to take the throne for himself. Adonijah, half-brother of Solomon and full brother of Absalom, "exalted himself, saying, I will be king: and he prepared him chariots and horsemen, and fifty men to run before him."

Then he invited the king's other sons to follow him "and all the men of Judah the king's servants," and many did so. "But Nathan the prophet, and Benaiah, and the mighty men, and Solomon his brother, he called not."

Sensing that Adonijah was creating a rebellion, Nathan the prophet went to Solomon's mother, Bathsheba, and said, "Hast thou not heard that Adonijah the son of Haggith [another of David's wives] doth reign, and David our lord knoweth it not?"

He sent her to the king to report what Adonijah was doing, and the king was deeply disturbed. Bathsheba said, "Now, behold, Adonijah reigneth; and now, my lord the king, thou knowest it not:

"And he hath slain oxen and fat cattle and sheep in abundance, and hath called all the sons of the king, and Abiathar the priest, and Joab the captain of the host: but Solomon thy servant hath he not called.

"And thou, my lord, O king, the eyes of all Israel are upon thee, that thou shouldest tell them who shall sit on the throne of my lord the king after him.

"Otherwise it shall come to pass, when my lord the king shall sleep with his fathers, that I and my son Solomon shall be counted offenders."

David immediately called in Zadock the priest and Nathan

the prophet and reaffirmed Solomon's appointment. They again
took oil and anointed Solomon king.

Adonijah was having a party with many guests. When they
heard that David had reconfirmed Solomon as his successor, "all
the guests that were with Adonijah were afraid, and rose up, and
went every man his way.

"And Adonijah feared because of Solomon, and arose, and
went, and caught hold on the horns of the altar. And it was told
Solomon, saying, Behold, Adonijah feareth king Solomon: for,
lo, he hath caught hold on the horns of the altar, saying, Let king
Solomon swear unto me to day that he will not slay his servant
with the sword.

"And Solomon said, If he will shew himself a worthy man,
there shall not an hair of him fall to the earth: but if wickedness
shall be found in him, he shall die."

King Solomon sent for Adonijah, and the son was brought
down from the altar. As he entered into Solomon's presence, he
"bowed himself to king Solomon: and Solomon said unto him,
Go to thine house. . . .

"Then sat Solomon upon the throne of David his father; and
his kingdom was established greatly.

"And Adonijah the son of Haggith came to Bath-sheba the
mother of Solomon. And she said, Comest thou peaceably? And
he said, Peaceably. He said moreover, I have somewhat to say
unto thee. And she said, Say on.

"And he said, Thou knowest that the kingdom was mine, and
that all Israel set their faces on me, that I should reign: howbeit
the kingdom is turned about, and is become my brother's: for it
was his from the Lord. And now I ask one petition of thee, deny
me not. And she said unto him, Say on.

"And he said, Speak, I pray thee, unto Solomon the king,
(for he will not say thee nay,) that he give me Abishag the
Shunammite to wife.

"And Bath-sheba said, Well; I will speak for thee unto the
king."

Bathsheba went to King Solomon, to speak for Adonijah.
"And the king rose up to meet her, and bowed himself unto her,
and sat down on his throne, and caused a seat to be set for the
king's mother; and she sat on his right hand.

"Then she said, I desire one small petition of thee; I pray thee, say me not nay. And the king said unto her, Ask on, my mother: for I will not say thee nay.

"And she said, Let Abishag the Shunammite be given to Adonijah thy brother to wife.

"And king Solomon answered and said unto his mother, And why dost thou ask Abishag the Shunammite for Adonijah? ask for him the kingdom also; for he is mine elder brother; even for him, and for Abiathar the priest, and for Joab the son of Zeruiah.

"Then king Solomon sware by the Lord, saying, God do so to me, and more also, if Adonijah have not spoken this word against his own life. Now therefore, as the Lord liveth, which hath established me, and set me on the throne of David my father, and who hath made me an house, as he promised, Adonijah shall be put to death this day.

"And king Solomon sent by the hand of Benaiah the son of Jehoiada; and he fell upon him that he died." (1 Kings 1; 2:12-25.)

Joab, who had been so faithful to David previously, was one of Adonijah's supporters. When he heard of Adonijah's death, he fled to the sanctuary for protection. But Solomon condemned him to death and the king's men "fell upon him, and slew him." (1 Kings 2:34.)

So ended this revolt against Solomon.

Chapter Thirty-three

THE DEATH OF DAVID

David, in his old age, knew that death was approaching. He called in Solomon and charged him: "I go the way of all the earth: be thou strong therefore, and shew thyself a man;

"And keep the charge of the Lord thy God, to walk in his ways, to keep his statutes, and his commandments, and his judgments, and his testimonies, as it is written in the law of Moses, that thou mayest prosper in all that thou doest, and whithersoever thou turnest thyself:

"That the Lord may continue his word which he spake concerning me, saying, If thy children take heed to their way, to walk before me in truth with all their heart and with all their soul, there shall not fail thee (said he) a man on the throne of Israel."

David then pleaded with his son on behalf of some of his followers:

"Moreover thou knowest also what Joab the son of Zeruiah did to me, and what he did to the two captains of the hosts of Israel, unto Abner the son of Ner, and unto Amasa the son of Jether, whom he slew, and shed the blood of war in peace, and put the blood of war upon his girdle that was about his loins, and in his shoes that were on his feet.

"Do therefore according to thy wisdom, and let not his hoar head go down to the grave in peace.

"But shew kindness unto the sons of Barzillai and Gileadite, and let them be of those that eat at thy table: for so they came to me when I fled because of Absalom thy brother.

"And, behold, thou hast with thee Shimei the son of Gera, a Benjamite of Bahurim, which cursed me with a grievous curse in the day when I went to Mahanaim: but he came down to meet me at Jordan, and I sware to him by the Lord, saying, I will not put thee to death with the sword.

"Now therefore hold him not guiltless: for thou art a wise

man, and knowest what thou oughtest to do unto him; but his hoar head bring thou down to the grave with blood.''

At the conclusion of this speech, the scripture says, "David slept with his fathers, and was buried in the city of David. And the days that David reigned over Israel were forty years: seven years reigned he in Hebron, and thirty and three years reigned he in Jerusalem.

"Then sat Solomon upon the throne of David his father; and his kingdom was established greatly." (1 Kings 2:2-12.)

Chapter Thirty-four

THE PSALMS
OF DAVID

David was one of the world's greatest poets, ancient or modern. Many of the psalms that he wrote in praise to God are in the book of Psalms in the Bible. Others were included in the main text of the Bible. All rank high in quality; some are superb. They are accepted as scripture, being incorporated in the Bible. Hence we regard them as being inspired.

The best-known of all the psalms is the twenty-third, which has now been incorporated in the rituals of some Christian denominations. Its beauty is unexcelled:

The Lord is my shepherd; I shall not want.

He maketh me to lie down in green pastures:

He leadeth me beside the still waters.

He restoreth my soul:

He leadeth me in the paths of righteousness

For his name's sake.

Yea, though I walk through the valley

Of the shadow of death,

I will fear no evil:

For thou art with me;

Thy rod and thy staff they comfort me.

Thou preparest a table before me

In the presence of mine enemies:

Thou anointest my head with oil;

My cup runneth over.

Surely goodness and mercy shall follow me

All the days of my life:

And I will dwell in the house of the Lord for ever.

Another psalm that inspires every reader is the twenty-fourth:

> The earth is the Lord's,
> And the fulness thereof;
> The world, and they that dwell therein.
> For he hath founded it upon the seas,
> And established it upon the floods.
> Who shall ascend into the hill of the Lord?
> Or who shall stand in his holy place?
> He that hath clean hands, and a pure heart;
> Who hath not lifted up his soul unto vanity,
> Nor sworn deceitfully.
> He shall receive the blessing from the Lord,
> And righteousness from the God of his salvation.
> This is the generation of them that seek him,
> That seek thy face, O Jacob. Selah.
> Lift up your heads, O ye gates;
> And be ye lift up, ye everlasting doors;
> And the King of glory shall come in.
> Who is this King of glory?
> The Lord strong and mighty,
> The Lord mighty in battle.
> Lift up your heads, O ye gates;
> Even lift them up, ye everlasting doors;
> And the King of glory shall come in.
> Who is this King of glory?
> The Lord of hosts,
> He is the King of glory. Selah.

The sentiment of one psalm is incorporated in a well-known hymn, "The Lord Is My Light." It is listed as the twenty-seventh psalm. The first verse reads:

> The Lord is my light and my salvation;
> Whom shall I fear?

The Lord is the strength of my life;

Of whom shall I be afraid?

In his deep distress David cries out to God in the sixteenth psalm: "Thou wilt not leave my soul in hell." His further repentance is shown in these words:

Blessed is he whose transgression is forgiven,

Whose sin is covered.

Blessed is the man unto whom the Lord

Imputeth not iniquity,

And in whose spirit there is no guile.

While I kept silence,

My bones waxed old through my roaring

All the day long.

For day and night thy hand was heavy upon me:

My moisture is turned into

The drought of summer. Selah.

I acknowledged my sin unto thee,

And mine iniquity have I not hid.

I said, I will confess my transgressions

Unto the Lord;

And thou forgavest the iniquity of my sin.

Selah. (Psalm 32:1-5.)

Further evidence of his regret is found in the thirty-eighth psalm, wherein David says:

O Lord, rebuke me not in thy wrath:

Neither chasten me in thy hot displeasure.

For thine arrows stick fast in me,

And thy hand presseth me sore.

There is no soundness in my flesh

Because of thine anger;

Neither is there any rest in my bones

Because of my sin.

For mine iniquities are gone over mine head:
As an heavy burden
They are too heavy for me. . . .
I am troubled;
I am bowed down greatly;
I go mourning all the day long. . . .
Lord, all my desire is before thee;
And my groaning is not hid from thee.
My heart panteth,
My strength faileth me:
As for the light of mine eyes,
It also is gone from me.

In his twenty-second psalm David cries out:

Why hast thou forsaken me?
Why art thou so far from helping me,
And from the words of my roaring?
O my God, I cry in the daytime,
But thou hearest not;
And in the night season,
And am not silent.
But thou art holy,
O thou that inhabitest the praises of Israel.
Our fathers trusted in thee:
They trusted, and thou didst deliver them.
They cried unto thee, and were delivered:
They trusted in thee, and were not confounded.
But I am a worm, and no man;
A reproach of men, and despised of the people.
All they that see me laugh me to scorn:
They shoot out the lip,
They shake the head.

In the fifty-third psalm he affirms:

The fool hath said in his heart,
There is no God.
Corrupt are they,
And have done abominable iniquity:
There is none that doeth good.

In this same psalm he speaks of apostasy:

God looked down from heaven
Upon the children of men,
To see if there were any that did understand,
That did seek God.
Every one of them is gone back:
They are altogether become filthy;
There is none that doeth good,
No, not one.
Have the workers of iniquity no knowledge?
Who eat up my people as they eat bread:
They have not called upon God.
There were they in great fear,
Where no fear was:
For God hath scattered the bones of him
That encampeth against thee:
Thou hast put them to shame,
Because God hath despised them.
Oh that the salvation of Israel
Were come out of Zion!
When God bringeth back
The captivity of his people,
Jacob shall rejoice,
And Israel shall be glad.

His psalm on the Creation, Psalm 104, is most impressive:

Bless the Lord, O my soul.
O Lord my God, thou art very great;

Thou art clothed with honour and majesty.
Who coverest thyself with light as with a garment:
Who stretchest out the heavens
Like a curtain:
Who layeth the beams of his chambers
In the waters:
Who maketh the clouds his chariot:
Who walketh upon the wings of the wind:
Who maketh his angels spirits;
His ministers a flaming fire:
Who laid the foundations of the earth,
That it should not be removed for ever.
Thou coveredst it with the deep as with a garment:
The waters stood above the mountains.
At thy rebuke they fled;
At the voice of thy thunder they hasted away.
They go up by the mountains;
They go down by the valleys
Unto the place which thou hast founded for them.
Thou hast set a bound that they may not pass over;
That they turn not again
To cover the earth.
He sendeth the springs into the valleys,
Which run among the hills.
They give drink to every beast of the field:
The wild asses quench their thirst.
By them shall the fowls of the heaven
Have their habitation,
Which sing among the branches.
He watereth the hills from his chambers:
The earth is satisfied
With the fruit of thy works.

He causeth the grass to grow for the cattle,
And herb for the service of man:
That he may bring forth food out of the earth;
And wine that maketh glad the heart of man,
And oil to make his face to shine,
And bread which strengtheneth man's heart.
The trees of the Lord are full of sap;
The cedars of Lebanon,
Which he hath planted;
Where the birds make their nests:
As for the stork,
The fir trees are her house.
The high hills are a refuge for the wild goats;
And the rocks for the conies.
He appointed the moon for seasons:
The sun knoweth his going down.
Thou makest darkness, and it is night:
Wherein all the beasts of the forest do creep forth.
The young lions roar after their prey,
And seek their meat from God.
The sun ariseth,
They gather themselves together,
And lay them down in their dens.
Man goeth forth unto his work
And to his labour until the evening.
O Lord, how manifold are thy works!
In wisdom hast thou made them all:
The earth is full of thy riches.

He adds beautifully to it with his eighth psalm. The three best-known verses are these (vss. 4-6):

What is man, that thou art mindful of him?
And the son of man, that thou visitest him?

For thou hast made him a little lower
Than the angels,
And hast crowned him with glory and honour.
Thou madest him to have dominion
Over the works of thy hands;
Thou hast put all things under his feet.

To the Savior David wrote Psalm 110, one of the most inspirational:

The Lord said unto my Lord,
Sit thou at my right hand,
Until I make thine enemies thy footstool.
The Lord shall send the rod of thy strength
Out of Zion:
Rule thou in the midst of thine enemies.
Thy people shall be willing in the day of thy power,
In the beauties of holiness
From the womb of the morning:
Thou hast the dew of thy youth.
The Lord hath sworn,
And will not repent,
Thou art a priest for ever
After the order of Melchizedek.
The Lord at thy right hand
Shall strike through kings
In the day of his wrath.
He shall judge among the heathen,
He shall fill the places with the dead bodies;
He shall wound the heads over many countries.
He shall drink of the brook in the way:
Therefore shall he lift up the head.

And with Psalm 110, Psalm 127 should be read:

Except the Lord build the house,

They labour in vain that build it:
Except the Lord keep the city,
The watchman waketh but in vain.
It is in vain for you to rise up early,
To sit up late,
To eat the bread of sorrows:
For so he giveth his beloved sleep.
Lo, children are an heritage of the Lord:
And the fruit of the womb is his reward.
As arrows are in the hand of a mighty man;
So are children of the youth.
Happy is the man that hath his quiver full of them:
They shall not be ashamed,
But they shall speak with the enemies
In the gate.

Some of David's finest classical language is found in Psalm 133:

Behold, how good and how pleasant it is
For brethren to dwell together in unity!
It is like the precious ointment
Upon the head,
That ran down upon the beard,
Even Aaron's beard:
That went down to the skirts of his garments;
As the dew of Hermon,
And as the dew that descended
Upon the mountains of Zion:
For there the Lord commanded the blessing,
Even life for evermore.

The language of the psalms is exquisite. Where did David receive the training necessary to produce these literary gems? What was the extent of his education?

The schools of Palestine in those days were nothing like ours of today. Could they have produced a Shakespeare? And David was greater than Shakespeare. Could they have produced a Tennyson or a Longfellow? These poets cannot be compared to David. He is in a class by himself.

What is the answer, then?

David was the beloved of the Lord. Despite his one tragic mistake, he nevertheless performed the work assigned to him. He is usually classed first of all as a warrior-king. But who can discount the inspiration in his writings? And what was the source of that inspiration?

Over and over again the scripture says the Spirit of the Lord was with David. Thence came his inspiration! He was taught by that Spirit!

The writings of the prophets had the same source. What was Isaiah's education, obtained in Palestine? Nothing to qualify him to write the works he produced. What school could have taught him sufficiently to write—of his own efforts—chapter 53 of his book, for example? Or chapter 2, or chapter 9? What school could have prepared him to write these words:

For unto us a child is born,

Unto us a son is given:

And the government

Shall be upon his shoulder:

And his name shall be called Wonderful,

Counseller, The mighty God,

The everlasting Father,

The Prince of Peace.

(Isaiah 9:6.)

And who on earth could have taught him to write the following:

And when they shall say unto you,

Seek unto them that have familiar spirits,

And unto wizards that peep,

And that mutter:

Should not a people seek unto their God?

For the living to the dead?

To the law and to the testimony:

If they speak not according to this word,

It is because there is no light in them.

(Isaiah 8:19-20.)

Or who could have taught him the thoughts expressed in chapter 14 of his book? Note these words and marvel:

How art thou fallen from heaven,

O Lucifer, son of the morning!

How art thou cut down to the ground,

Which didst weaken the nations!

For thou hast said in thine heart,

I will ascend into heaven,

I will exalt my throne above the stars of God:

I will sit also upon

The mount of the congregation,

In the sides of the north:

I will ascend above the heights of the clouds;

I will be like the most High.

Yet thou shalt be brought down to hell,

To the sides of the pit.

They that see thee shall narrowly look upon thee,

And consider thee, saying,

Is this the man that made the earth to tremble,

That did shake kingdoms;

That made the world as a wilderness,

And destroyed the cities thereof;

That opened not the house of his prisoners?

And Job—who taught him? No one with any existing literary work can surpass these inspired words:

Where wast thou when I laid

The foundations of the earth?

Declare, if thou hast understanding.

Who hath laid the measures thereof,

If thou knowest?

Or who hath stretched the line upon it?

Whereupon are the foundations thereof fastened?

Or who laid the corner stone thereof;

When the morning stars sang together,

And all the sons of God shouted for joy?

(Job 38:4-7.)

Or who taught Ezekiel to write with such wonderful diction? Not the schools of his day. He was the mouthpiece of God and was taught by the Spirit as were the other great prophets. Their works all came through the inspiration of heaven.

Like Joshua, in whose footsteps he trod, David also was a mighty warrior; but he also communed with God as did any other true prophet, and he received divine direction.

His writings were inspired of the Holy Spirit even as were those of Isaiah and Ezekiel. They certainly are not the product of his own mind nor of the schools that were available in that remote day in Palestine.

These writings are scripture. Scripture is in a class by itself. It is the dictation of the Spirit of God, and God is infinite.

PART IV
KING SOLOMON:
SON OF DAVID

*"And God gave Solomon wisdom
and understanding exceeding much,
and largeness of heart, even as the sand that is
on the sea shore. And Solomon's wisdom excelled the
wisdom of all the children of the east country, and all
the wisdom of Egypt." (1 Kings 4:29-30.)*

Chapter Thirty-five

THE KINGLY CONTRASTS

Completely different from both David and Saul, Solomon now reigned in Israel. His kingdom became the talk of the world, his wisdom the envy of all mankind. His wealth was beyond compare, and peace prevailed in his kingdom.

His reign began far more auspiciously than that of either of his predecessors. Saul had come to the throne in the midst of severe oppression by the Philistines. Also, he was an unknown. When Samuel presented him to the people, it seemed that Saul's stature was the only thing that greatly impressed them. He was head and shoulders taller than anyone else and looked the part of both a king and a warrior. The people liked that. But they did not know him. They knew nothing of his attitude, his skills, or his training. They took him almost entirely on Samuel's word.

It was not so with Solomon, who was raised in the royal court, and who enjoyed the love and admiration of the multitude. He was given every advantage that David, his successful father, could bestow upon him. But far beyond that, he was blessed of the Lord as no other king ever was.

Saul had been a herder of flocks. Nothing is said about any amount of wealth he may have had, if any. Following his choice as king he still continued to tend his father's flocks for a time. That would indicate a moderate living standard at most.

Solomon lived in the lap of luxury, a favored son in the royal palace, with servants everywhere to wait upon him.

Saul came to power in the midst of war, and almost immediately after his accession he had to lead his people out to battle.

Solomon arose in a time of peace. His father had provided that advantage for him. Through his military skill and the strength of his million-man army, David had finally accomplished what Joshua had set out to do. The enemy had been either destroyed or subdued. Now Israel had full control of Palestine. Her wealth was extensive too, largely acquired through conquest of the neighboring nations.

The contrast with his father was equally great for Solomon. David had been a man of war; Solomon was a man of peace. It took war to defeat the enemies of Israel. It took war to unite the Twelve Tribes into one nation and put down insurrection within their ranks. In battle David was supreme.

It required the sword and an iron will to search out enemies from within, the dissenters, the ambitious ones who aspired to become king, and those who would have taken the lives of David and Solomon. This included rebellion even within David's own family.

So it was David who had brought the kingdom up to a point of high respect among the neighboring nations, with the establishment of peace that resulted from it. It was David who had united the kingdom. It was he who had defeated the enemy. It was he who had brought prosperity to Israel and released her from the oppression of the Philistines. And more than that, it was David who had made extensive preparations for the building of the temple, although he was not allowed to build it himself.

All of this Solomon received as a gift from his father. The success of his reign seemed assured from the very beginning.

One thing was common to both David and Solomon, however, and it became the downfall of each. That was love for forbidden women.

As for Saul, women had not been very important in his life—until near the end. But then he demanded a woman, one who was a spiritualist medium, a necromancer, one who peeps and mutters. His need for her was to call up occult powers to guide him through his last dreadful days on earth.

David had wanted only one forbidden woman, another man's wife. For her he lost his exaltation in the kingdom of heaven. (D&C 132:39.)

Saul also had wanted only one forbidden woman, but she was a witch.

Solomon wanted many forbidden women, even idolaters for whom he built pagan shrines, and at least one of a race restricted for marriage by divine decree. Flying in the face of the Lord's prohibitions, Solomon, too, was rejected of God.

So the contrasts between Saul, Solomon, and David in the matter of women was great indeed.

They were three great kings, each in his own way. Each was strong, but also weak. Selfish emotion in all three opened the door to sheer tragedy.

Chapter Thirty-six

SOLOMON SEES GOD

On two different occasions King Solomon saw Almighty God. The first instance was when he began his reign. Wishing to help him in every way, the Lord came down and asked what gifts he would desire of heaven to assure a successful regime. How great was the condescension of God that he would do this!

The Lord said to the king: "Ask what I shall give thee."

Solomon replied, "Thou hast shewed great mercy unto David my father, and hast made me to reign in his stead. Now, O Lord God, let thy promise unto David my father be established: for thou hast made me king over a people like the dust of the earth in multitude. Give me now wisdom and knowledge, that I may go out and come in before this people: for who can judge this thy people, that is so great?"

And God said, "Because this was in thine heart, and thou hast not asked riches, wealth, or honour, nor the life of thine enemies, neither yet hast asked long life; but hast asked wisdom and knowledge for thyself, that thou mayest judge my people, over whom I have made thee king:

"Wisdom and knowledge is granted unto thee; and I will give thee riches, and wealth, and honour, such as none of the kings have had that have been before thee, neither shall there any after thee have the like." (2 Chronicles 1:7-12.)

Although Solomon's court visitors included the great rulers of the earth, the king was mindful also of the lowliest of his subjects.

One day two women came to him, disputing over their children. One of the women said, "O my lord, I and this woman dwell in one house; and I was delivered of a child with her in the house.

"And it came to pass the third day after that I was delivered, that this woman was delivered also: and we were together; there was no stranger with us in the house, save we two in the house.

"And this woman's child died in the night; because she overlaid it.

"And she arose at midnight, and took my son from beside me, while thine handmaid slept, and laid it in her bosom, and laid her dead child in my bosom.

"And when I rose in the morning to give my child suck, behold, it was dead: but when I had considered it in the morning, behold, it was not my son, which I did bear."

The other woman denied the accusation: "Nay; but the living is my son, and the dead is thy son."

Solomon, after listening to both sides, told his servants to bring him a sword. Then he said, "Divide the living child in two, and give half to the one, and half to the other.

"Then spake the woman whose the living child was unto the king, for her bowels yearned upon her son, and she said, O my lord, give her the living child, and in no wise slay it. But the other said, Let it be neither mine nor thine, but divide it.

"Then the king answered and said, Give her the living child, and in no wise slay it: she is the mother thereof.

"And all Israel heard of the judgment which the king had judged; and they feared the king: for they saw that the wisdom of God was in him, to do judgment." (1 Kings 3:17-28.)

Chapter Thirty-seven

THE QUEEN OF SHEBA

Famed as he was for his wealth and power, Solomon was best known for his wisdom. Truly the Lord's promise was fulfilled abundantly when he said to the king, "wisdom and knowledge is granted unto you."

One example of this is found in the visit of the queen of Sheba. For years Bible critics thought that this biblical story was a myth, but now archaeologists have proven otherwise. There was a queen of Sheba, and there is evidence of her visit to Solomon.

"When the queen of Sheba heard of the fame of Solomon, she came to prove Solomon with hard questions at Jerusalem, with a very great company, and camels that bare spices, and gold in abundance, and precious stones: and when she was come to Solomon, she communed with him of all that was in her heart.

"And Solomon told her all her questions: and there was nothing hid from Solomon which he told her not.

"And when the queen of Sheba had seen the wisdom of Solomon, and the house that he had built, and the meat of his table, and the sitting of his servants, and the attendance of his ministers, and their apparel; his cupbearers also, and their apparel; and his ascent by which he went up into the house of the Lord; there was no more spirit in her."

The queen then said to Solomon, "It was a true report which I heard in mine own land of thine acts, and of thy wisdom: Howbeit I believed not their words, until I came, and mine eyes had seen it: and, behold, the one half of the greatness of thy wisdom was not told me: for thou exceedest the fame that I heard.

"Happy are thy men, and happy are these thy servants, which stand continually before thee, and hear thy wisdom.

"Blessed be the Lord thy God, which delighted in thee to set thee on his throne, to be king for the Lord thy God: because thy

God loved Israel, to establish them for ever, therefore made he thee king over them, to do judgment and justice.

"And she gave the king an hundred and twenty talents of gold, and of spices great abundance, and precious stones: neither was there any such spice as the queen of Sheba gave king Solomon.'' (2 Chronicles 9:1-9.)

Who was this queen of Sheba? And what was Sheba? Was it a city, a country? Where was it?

Archaeologists have found that Sheba was a kingdom in what today is known as Yemen, south and west of Saudi Arabia. It is on the Red Sea facing Africa at a point where the Gulf of Aden and the Red Sea merge. It reached its political and historical zenith about 1000 B.C.

Werner Keller in his book *The Bible as History* refers to writings of the ninth century B.C. relating to the Kingdom of Minaea, in what is now the northern part of modern Yemen. They speak of a southern neighbor, the land of the Shebans. Assyrian documents of the eighth century B.C. also make reference to the Shebans. Keller says this:

"Gradually, with the discovery of documentary evidence, this fairy-tale country of Sheba began to take definite shape.

"A gigantic dam blocked the River Adhanat in Sheba, collecting the rainfall from a wide area. The water was then led off into canals for irrigation purposes, which was what gave the land its fertility. Remains of this technical marvel in the shape of walls over sixty feet high still defy the sand dunes of the desert. Just as Holland is in modern times the Land of Tulips, so Sheba was then the Land of Spices, one vast fairy-like scented garden of the costliest spices in the world.

"In the midst of it lay the capital, which was called Marib. For 1500 years this garden of spices bloomed around Marib. That was until 542 B.C. Then the dam burst. The importunate desert crept over the fertile lands and destroyed them.

" 'The people of Sheba,' says the Koran, 'had beautiful gardens in which the most costly fruits ripened.' But then the people turned their backs upon God, wherefor he punished them by causing the dam to burst. Thereafter nothing but bitter fruit grew in the gardens of Sheba.'' (New York: William Morrow and Co., 1956, p. 209.)

Archaeologists for a time excavated the old Sheban capital of Marib and found there an oval-shaped temple three hundred feet long. It was a shrine to the moon-god Ilumquh. There was a pillared hall in the inner court. Stone pillars fifteen feet high still stand there, having been supported and preserved over the centuries by the sand dunes that drifted about them. The hostility of the governor of Marib stopped the excavations.

Speaking of the queen of Sheba who visited Solomon, Keller asserts that the biblical description of her visit ''rings true and is completely intelligible.''

So there was a Sheba; it had a queen, and her visit to Solomon is entirely within the facts that archaeologists are now beginning to unearth.

Chapter Thirty-eight

SOLOMON'S WEALTH

King Solomon did nothing in a small way. He was what we of today would call a "big-time operator."

His wealth was fabulous, most of it obtained as tribute from nations now subject to him. Much was developed within Palestine itself, however, such as in the extensive mining and processing of copper and iron, even for export.

Solomon was a spender. He had much and he spent much, and all of his planning was on a gigantic scale. For example, he had "a thousand and four hundred chariots, and twelve thousand horsemen, which he placed in the chariot cities, and with the king at Jerusalem. And the king made silver and gold at Jerusalem as plenteous as stones, and cedar trees made he as the sycomore trees that are in the vale for abundance.

"And Solomon had horses brought out of Egypt, and linen yarn: the king's merchants received the linen yarn at a price.

"And they fetched up, and brought forth out of Egypt a chariot for six hundred shekels of silver, and an horse for a hundred and fifty: and so brought they out horses for all the kings of the Hittites, and for the kings of Syria, by their means." (2 Chronicles 1:14-17.)

When he prepared to build the temple he planned the most beautiful structure he could devise. When he called men to labor on it, he summoned "threescore and ten thousand men to bear burdens, and fourscore thousand to hew in the mountain, and three thousand and six hundred to oversee them." (2 Chronicles 2:2.) That many supervisors surely would get the job done.

When he offered sacrifices to the Lord, again it was no small matter. "Solomon offered a sacrifice of peace offerings, which he offered unto the Lord, two and twenty thousand oxen, and an hundred and twenty thousand sheep." (1 Kings 8:63.)

Solomon did much international trading, including the use of overseas shipping, with many varied cargoes coming from distant ports. He "made a navy of ships in Ezion-geber, which is beside Eloth, on the shore of the Red Sea, in the land of Edom.

"And Hiram sent in the navy his servants, shipmen that had knowledge of the sea, with the servants of Solomon. And they came to Ophir, and fetched from thence gold, four hundred and twenty talents, and brought it to king Solomon. . . .

"And all king Solomon's drinking vessels were of gold, and all the vessels of the house of the forest of Lebanon were of pure gold; none were of silver: it was nothing accounted of in the days of Solomon.

"For the king had at sea a navy of Tharshish with the navy of Hiram: once in three years came the navy of Tharshish, bringing gold, and silver, ivory, and apes, and peacocks." (1 Kings 9:26-28; 10:21-22.)

It is interesting that he imported such things as apes and peacocks, to say nothing of ivory and precious metals. The wealth of surrounding nations seemed to flow with ease to Solomon. Of course many of the kings paid him rich peace offerings, for David had conquered them, and they now were subject to Solomon.

"Now the weight of gold that came to Solomon in one year was six hundred and threescore and six talents of gold; Beside that which chapmen and merchants brought. And all the kings of Arabia and governors of the country brought gold and silver to Solomon.

"And king Solomon made two hundred targets of beaten gold: six hundred shekels of beaten gold went to one target. And three hundred shields made he of beaten gold: three hundred shekels of gold went to one shield. And the king put them in the house of the forest of Lebanon.

"Moreover the king made a great throne of ivory, and overlaid it with pure gold.

"And there were six steps to the throne, with a footstool of gold, which were fastened to the throne, and stays on each side of the sitting place, and two lions standing by the stays: And twelve lions stood there on the one side and on the other upon the six steps. There was not the like made in any kingdom."

With all his possessions, the Bible tells us, "King Solomon

passed all the kings of the earth in riches and wisdom.''

Moreover, ''all the kings of the earth sought the presence of Solomon, to hear his wisdom, that God had put in his heart. And they brought every man his present, vessels of silver, and vessels of gold, and raiment, harness, and spices, horses, and mules, a rate year by year.

''And Solomon had four thousand stalls for horses and chariots, and twelve thousand horsemen; whom he bestowed in the chariot cities, and with the king of Jerusalem.

''And he reigned over all the kings from the river even unto the land of the Philistines, and to the border of Egypt.'' (2 Chronicles 9:13-26.)

But perhaps even more important than his wealth is this: ''And all the earth sought to Solomon, to hear his wisdom, which God had put in his heart.''

God seemed to withhold nothing from Solomon. Obviously his was the most fabulous regime in all history for Israel.

Chapter Thirty-nine

SOLOMON'S COPPER INDUSTRY

With the knowledge and wisdom God had bestowed upon him, and through his contacts with other nations, Solomon developed the Promised Land industrially for the first time.

Throughout the centuries Palestine had been pastoral. It was so in the days of the Savior too, for by that time industrialization as Solomon knew it had disappeared. The people were back on the land with their sheep and their olive trees.

But with his wealth and knowledge Solomon greatly changed his nation. As has been noted, he opened large mining operations. When it is considered that he employed ''threescore and ten thousand men to bear burdens, and fourscore thousand to hew in the mountain, and three thousand and six hundred to oversee them'' (2 Chronicles 2:2), it is seen that he went into his projects in a large way.

Many of the men who ''hewed in the mountain'' undoubtedly were miners. Some cut timber there for the king, and others worked in quarries where blocks and slabs of building stone were produced.

For centuries copper had been used by Israel. It was one of the first metals known in antiquity. It was soft and easily handled. The artisans of those days learned that by mixing it with tin, they would produce a hardened metal that they called brass, but which modern experts say was really bronze. It will be remembered that brass was known in Genesis, for Tubalcain was an instructor in the use of both brass and iron. (Genesis 4:22.)

When Moses described the beauties of the Promised Land to the people he led out of Egypt, he spoke of it as ''a land wherein thou shalt eat bread without scarceness, thou shalt not lack any thing in it; a land whose stones are iron, and out of whose hills thou mayest dig brass. '' (Deuteronomy 8:9.)

It is believed that reference to brass in this passage in fact meant copper or bronze. Modern experts say that the brass we know today is an alloy of zinc and copper, and that zinc was not known in Palestine in Bible times. However, both copper and tin were known, and, combined, they make bronze.

When Canaan was conquered by the Israelites, they kept to the hill country, leaving the sea coasts largely to the Philistines and Phoenicians. It was in these hills where they found metal.

For years the Bible critics felt that the story of Solomon's mines was another bit of mythology. But now, as with the queen of Sheba, archaeology has proven the critics wrong. It has shown that Solomon did have both iron and copper mines, and that he processed these metals as well. Even the blast furnaces of Solomon have been found.

Keller, in his *The Bible as History* (p. 197), says that the smelters in Palestine under Solomon were at Ezion-geber, which he calls "the Pittsburgh of old Palestine." Then, in his excellent work, he says:

"King Solomon, whom Glueck describes as the 'great copper king,' must probably be reckoned among the greatest exporters of copper in the ancient world. Research on other sites completes the picture of Palestine's economy under King Solomon. South of the old Philistine city of Gaza, Flinders Petrie dug up iron-smelting installations in Wadi Ghazze. The furnaces were like those at Tell el Kheleifeh, but smaller.

"David had disputed the Philistines' right to their monopoly of iron, and he had extracted their secret smelting process as one of the prices of their defeat. Then under Solomon the iron and copper deposits were mined on a large scale and smelted."

William Neal, in his book *The Bible Companion* (p. 392) says: "Foreign trade did not really begin until David made himself overlord of the surrounding territories of Philistia, Moab, Ammon, and Edom. This opened up the trade-routes to Tyre in the north, Egypt in the southwest, and the Red Sea in the south.

"Under Solomon, trading with these countries greatly increased. Solomon bought horses from Cilicia and Cappadocia and sold them to Egypt, using money to buy chariots in Egypt for sale to Cilicia and Cappadocia. He exported food, mainly to Tyre, receiving in exchange men and materials for building his Temple, and sailors to man the ships which sailed from Ezion-geber on the Red Sea to Ophir. These ships exported Ezion-geber's production of copper and iron, and brought back in return 'gold and silver, ivory, apes and peacocks.' (1 Kings 10:22.)''

This same reference also says: ''Solomon had a monopoly on foreign trade. In addition he exercised the right of every power lying athwart a trade route, and levied tolls on all the merchants passing through his territory.'' (1 Kings 10:14-15.)

So Solomon's wisdom was not limited to giving advice to people in trouble, nor to foreign ambassadors and rulers who visited his court, nor even to writing proverbs. He used his divinely bestowed knowledge and wisdom in business and industry as well. Never, before Solomon or since, has Palestine known such expansion into fields long thought to be foreign to her.

With Solomon's wisdom and tremendous insight in both industry and international trade, it is no wonder that kings from afar came to visit him. Their trips naturally would have been at least partially business-related to sustain the trading and bartering that went on during those days.

Chapter Forty

THE TEMPLE
IS BUILT

David had given Solomon a direct charge to build a temple to the Lord, and the Almighty himself confirmed it. David was not allowed to erect it, for he was "a man of blood." But Solomon, his son, was given this privilege.

David had brought peace to Palestine. There were no more wars in any part of the kingdom, nor internal insurrection, nor attacks from the Canaanites outside. Even the Philistines were subdued.

"And Hiram king of Tyre sent his servants unto Solomon; for he had heard that they had anointed him king in the room of his father: for Hiram was ever a lover of David.

"And Solomon sent to Hiram, saying, Thou knowest how that David my father could not build an house unto the name of the Lord his God for the wars which were about him on every side, until the Lord put them under the soles of his feet.

"But now the Lord my God hath given me rest on every side, so that there is neither adversary nor evil occurrent. And, behold, I purpose to build an house unto the name of the Lord my God, as the Lord spake unto David my father, saying, Thy son, whom I will set upon thy throne in thy room, he shall build an house unto my name.

"Now therefore command thou that they hew me cedar trees out of Lebanon; and my servants shall be with thy servants: and unto thee will I give hire for thy servants according to all that thou shalt appoint: for thou knowest that there is not among us any that can skill to hew timber like unto the Sidonians."

When Hiram heard Solomon's words, he rejoiced greatly, and said, "Blessed be the Lord this day, which hath given unto David a wise son over this great people."

Then Hiram sent for Solomon, saying, "I have considered the things which thou sentest to me for: and I will do all thy desire concerning timber of cedar, and concerning timber of fir. My servants shall bring them down from Lebanon unto the sea: and I will convey them by sea in floats unto the place that thou shalt appoint me, and will cause them to be discharged there, and thou shalt receive them: and thou shalt accomplish my desire, in giving food for my household.

"So Hiram gave Solomon cedar trees and fir trees according to all his desire. And Solomon gave Hiram twenty thousand measures of wheat for food to his household, and twenty measures of pure oil: thus gave Solomon to Hiram year by year.

"And the Lord gave Solomon wisdom, as he promised him: and there was peace between Hiram and Solomon; and they two made a league together."

Solomon then called up thirty thousand men from the various tribes of Israel and assigned them to go to Lebanon to produce building material for the temple. "And he sent them to Lebanon, ten thousand a month by courses: a month they were in Lebanon, and two months at home: and Adoniram was over the levy.

"And Solomon had threescore and ten thousand that bare burdens, and fourscore thousand hewers in the mountains; Beside the chief of Solomon's officers which were over the work, three thousand and three hundred, which ruled over the people that wrought in the work.

"And the king commanded, and they brought great stones, costly stones, and hewed stones, to lay the foundation of the house.

"And Solomon's builders and Hiram's builders did hew them, and the stonesquarers: so they prepared timber and stones to build the house." (1 Kings 5.)

The temple was to be approximately one hundred feet long and forty feet wide, and fifty feet high at its tallest point. A front porch about thirty-five feet long, the breadth of the house, was also provided. The temple was approximately the size of our modern temples.

"And the house, when it was in building, was built of stone made ready before it was brought thither: so that there was neither hammer nor axe nor any tool of iron heard in the house, while it was in building. . . .

"And the cedar of the house within was carved with knops

and open flowers: all was cedar; there was no stone seen.

"And the oracle he prepared in the house within, to set there the ark of the covenant of the Lord. And the oracle in the forepart was twenty cubits in length, and twenty cubits in breadth, and twenty cubits in the height thereof: and he overlaid it with pure gold; and so covered the altar which was of cedar.

"So Solomon overlaid the house within with pure gold: and he made a partition by the chains of gold before the oracle; and he overlaid it with gold. And the whole house he overlaid with gold, until he had finished all the house: also the whole altar that was by the oracle he overlaid with gold. . . .

"And for the entering of the oracle he made doors of olive tree: the lintel and side posts were a fifth part of the wall.

"The two doors also were of olive tree; and he carved upon them carvings of cherubims and palm trees and open flowers, and overlaid them with gold, and spread gold upon the cherubims, and upon the palm trees.

"So also made he for the door of the temple posts of olive tree, a fourth part of the wall.

"And the two doors were of fir tree: the two leaves of the one door were folding, and the two leaves of the other door were folding.

"And he carved thereon cherubims and palm trees and open flowers: and covered them with gold fitted upon the carved work. . . .

"In the fourth year was the foundation of the house of the Lord laid, in the month Zif: And in the eleventh year, in the month of Bul, which is the eighth month, was the house finished throughout all the parts thereof, and according to all the fashion of it. So was he seven years in building it." (1 Kings 6.)

Numerous vessels pertaining to the temple were manufactured.

"And he made a molten sea, ten cubits from the one brim to the other: it was round all about, and his height was five cubits: and a line of thirty cubits did compass it round about. . . .

"It stood upon twelve oxen, three looking toward the north, and three looking toward the west, and three looking toward the south, and three looking toward the east: and the sea was set above upon them, and all their hinder parts were inward. . . .

"And the pots, and the shovels, and the basons: and all these vessels, which Hiram made to king Solomon for the house of the Lord, were of bright brass. . . . And Solomon left all the vessels unweighed, because they were exceeding many: neither was the weight of the brass found out.

"And Solomon made all the vessels that pertained unto the house of the Lord: the altar of gold, and the table of gold, where-upon the shewbread was, And the candlesticks of pure gold, five on the right side, and five on the left, before the oracle, with the flowers, and the lamps, and the tongs of gold, And the bowls, and the snuffers, and the basons, and the spoons, and the censers of pure gold; and the hinges of gold, both for the doors of the inner house, the most holy place, and for the doors of the house, to wit, of the temple.

"So was ended all the work that king Solomon made for the house of the Lord. And Solomon brought in the things which David his father had dedicated; even the silver, and the gold, and the vessels, did he put among the treasures of the house of the Lord." (1 Kings 7.)

Then Solomon built his own palace, virtually as large as the temple and quite as elaborate. Thirteen years were required to build it, compared to seven years for the temple.

Chapter Forty-one

THE ARK
IS PLACED

The ark of the covenant had been kept in a tentlike tabernacle through the years. Now it was the intention of the Lord that it should be placed within the new temple, "in the most holy place."

"Then Solomon assembled the elders of Israel, and all the heads of the tribes, the chief of the fathers of the children of Israel, unto king Solomon in Jerusalem, that they might bring up the ark of the covenant of the Lord out of the city of David, which is Zion. . . .

"And they brought up the ark of the Lord, and the tabernacle of the congregation, and all the holy vessels that were in the tabernacle, even those did the priests and the Levites bring up.

"And king Solomon, and all the congregation of Israel, that were assembled unto him, were with him before the ark, sacrificing sheep and oxen, that could not be told nor numbered for multitude.

"And the priests brought in the ark of the covenant of the Lord unto his place, into the oracle of the house, to the most holy place, even under the wings of the cherubims.

"For the cherubims spread forth their two wings over the place of the ark, and the cherubims covered the ark and the staves thereof above.

"And they drew out the staves, that the ends of the staves were seen out in the holy place before the oracle, and they were not seen without: and there they are unto this day.

"There was nothing in the ark save the two tables of stone, which Moses put there at Horeb, when the Lord made a covenant with the children of Israel, when they came out of the land of Egypt.

"And it came to pass, when the priests were come out of the holy place, that the cloud filled the house of the Lord, So that the priests could not stand to minister because of the cloud: for the glory of the Lord had filled the house of the Lord.'' (1 Kings 8:1-11.)

The ark had passed through a troublous history, being carried about on a cart wherever it was taken. It was captured by the Philistines in battle and kept by them until the curse of the Lord made it impossible for them to hold it longer. Then it was sent back to Israel amid the rejoicing of the tribes, who still were sorely afflicted by their enemies.

All during the time of David, he desired to build a permanent place for the ark, but the Lord would not allow it. The ark was to be placed in a temple, and David was not permitted to erect that structure. Solomon had been chosen for that. Now the temple was built and the ark was safely placed within its "most holy place," as intended by the Lord.

The ark was very significant to Israel, for, as the scriptures indicate, it contained the covenant of the Lord that he made with the children of Israel when he brought them out of the land of Egypt.

Chapter Forty-two

THE TEMPLE DEDICATION

A multitude of Israel gathered together for the dedication of the temple. Solomon himself offered the prayer. As he addressed the heavens, he prayed:

"Lord God of Israel, there is no God like thee, in heaven above, or on earth beneath, who keepest covenant and mercy with thy servants that walk before thee with all their heart:

"Who hast kept with thy servant David my father that thou promisedst him: thou spakest also with thy mouth, and hast fulfilled it with thine hand, as it is this day.

"Therefore now, Lord God of Israel, keep with thy servant David my father that thou promisedst him, saying, There shall not fail thee a man in my sight to sit on the throne of Israel; so that thy children take heed to their way, that they walk before me as thou hast walked before me.

"And now, O God of Israel, let thy word, I pray thee, be verified, which thou spakest unto thy servant David my father.

"But will God indeed dwell on the earth? behold, the heaven and heaven of heavens cannot contain thee; how much less this house that I have builded?

"Yet have thou respect unto the prayer of thy servant, and to his supplication, O Lord my God, to hearken unto the cry and to the prayer, which thy servant prayeth before thee to day." (1 Kings 8:23-28.)

The entire prayer may be read in the book of First Kings.

Then the king, "and all Israel with him, offered sacrifice before the Lord. And Solomon offered a sacrifice of peace offerings, which he offered unto the Lord. . . . So the king and all the children of Israel dedicated the house of the Lord.

"The same day did the king hallow the middle of the court that was before the house of the Lord: for there he offered burnt offerings, and meat offerings, and the fat of the peace offerings:

because the brasen altar that was before the Lord was too little to receive the burnt offerings, and meat offerings, and the fat of the peace offerings.

"And at that time Solomon held a feast, and all Israel with him, a great congregation, from the entering in of Hamath unto the river of Egypt, before the Lord our God, seven days and seven days, even fourteen days.

"On the eighth day he sent the people away: and they blessed the king, and went unto their tents joyful and glad of heart for all the goodness that the Lord had done for David his servant, and for Israel his people." (1 Kings 8:62-66.)

Chapter Forty-three

SOLOMON'S SIN AND DEATH

No king had been so abundantly blessed as was Solomon. No people had experienced such a reign as his. But now the Lord came a second time to Solomon cautioning him because of the king's misdeeds. He said:

"I have heard thy prayer and thy supplication, that thou hast made before me: I have hallowed this house, which thou hast built, to put my name there for ever; and mine eyes and mine heart shall be there perpetually.

"And if thou wilt walk before me, as David thy father walked, in integrity of heart, and in uprightness, to do according to all that I have commanded thee, and wilt keep my statutes and my judgments:

"Then I will establish the throne of thy kingdom upon Israel for ever, as I promised to David thy father, saying, There shall not fail thee a man upon the throne of Israel.

"But if ye shall at all turn from following me, ye or your children, and will not keep my commandments and my statutes which I have set before you, but go and serve other gods, and worship them:

"Then will I cut off Israel out of the land which I have given them; and this house, which I have hallowed for my name, will I cast out of my sight; and Israel shall be a proverb and a byword among all people:

"And at this house, which is high, every one that passeth by it shall be astonished, and shall hiss; and they shall say, Why hath the Lord done thus unto this land, and to this house?

"And they shall answer, Because they forsook the Lord their God, who brought forth their fathers out of the land of Egypt, and have taken hold upon other gods, and have worshipped them, and served them: therefore hath the Lord brought upon them all this evil." (1 Kings 9:3-9.)

This frightful warning to the mighty monarch was no different from warnings given Israel previously, from Moses' day on down. It was the same as was given in Book of Mormon times. It is the same today. If the Lord's people will serve him faithfully, they will be blessed. Otherwise distress awaits them.

It was a timely warning, too, for Solomon already had begun to drift into forbidden paths. It seems incredible that a man who had been so blessed, and who had been visited twice by the Lord, would go astray.

Solomon had a thousand wives and concubines and he "loved many strange women." (1 Kings 11:1.) Many came from nations against which God had raised complete prohibitions, telling Israel not to contract marriages with them for fear they would lead the people of promise into false religions. The Lord had spoken plainly and deliberately:

"Neither shalt thou make marriages with them; thy daughter thou shalt not give unto his son, nor his daughter shalt thou take unto thy son.

"For they will turn away thy son from following me, that they may serve other gods: so will the anger of the Lord be kindled against you, and destroy thee suddenly.

"But thus shall ye deal with them; ye shall destroy their altars, and break down their images, and cut down their groves, and burn their graven images with fire.

"For thou art an holy people unto the Lord thy God: the Lord thy God hath chosen thee to be a special people unto himself, above all people that are upon the face of the earth." (Deuteronomy 7:3-6.)

He also spoke with equal force when he said:

"The graven images of their gods shall ye burn with fire: thou shalt not desire the silver or gold that is on them, nor take it unto thee, lest thou be snared therein: for it is an abomination to the Lord thy God.

"Neither shalt thou bring an abomination into thine house, lest thou be a cursed thing like it: but thou shalt utterly detest it, and thou shalt utterly abhor it; for it is a cursed thing." (Deuteronomy 7:25-26.)

Some of Solomon's wives were from Moab, some from Edom; some were Ammonites, Zidonians, and Hittites. And one of his favorites was one from Egypt. Pharaoh had given one of his daughters to Solomon, who favored her and even built an expensive house for her.

Unlawful as it was to marry them, the king also set up pagan shrines for these women—another sin denounced by the Lord—where these foreigners worshipped their idols. His wives turned away his heart "after other gods: and his heart was not perfect with the Lord his God, as was the heart of David his father.

"For Solomon went after Ashtoreth the goddess of the Zidonians, and after Milcom the abomination of the Ammonites. And Solomon did evil in the sight of the Lord, and went not fully after the Lord, as did David his father.

"Then did Solomon build an high place for Chemosh, the abomination of Moab, in the hill that is before Jerusalem, and for Molech, the abomination of the children of Ammon. And likewise did he for all his strange wives, which burnt incense and sacrificed unto their gods."

The Lord was intensely angry with Solomon, since he had specifically commanded "that he should not go after other gods: but he kept not that which the Lord commanded."

Again the Lord spoke sharply to Solomon, and this time announced that as punishment he would take the kingdom away from Solomon's family. Said he: "Forasmuch as this is done of thee, and thou hast not kept my covenant and my statutes, which I have commanded thee, I will surely rend the kingdom from thee, and will give it to thy servant.

"Notwithstanding in thy days I will not do it for David thy father's sake: but I will rend it out of the hand of thy son.

"Howbeit I will not rend away all the kingdom; but will give one tribe to thy son for David my servant's sake, and for Jerusalem's sake which I have chosen."

The Lord now raised up adversaries to Solomon. Among them was Jeroboam, the son of a widow who served in the palace.

"And this was the cause that he lifted up his hand against the king: Solomon built Millo, and repaired the breaches of the city of David his father.

"And the man Jeroboam was a mighty man of valour: and

Solomon seeing the young man that he was industrious, he made him ruler over all the charge of the house of Joseph.

"And it came to pass at that time when Jeroboam went out of Jerusalem, that the prophet Ahijah the Shilonite found him in the way; and he had clad himself with a new garment; and they two were alone in the field:

"And Ahijah caught the new garment that was on him, and rent it in twelve pieces:

"And he said to Jeroboam, Take thee ten pieces: for thus saith the Lord, the God of Israel, Behold, I will rend the kingdom out of the hand of Solomon, and will give ten tribes to thee:

"(But he shall have one tribe for my servant David's sake, and for Jerusalem's sake, the city which I have chosen out of all the tribes of Israel:)

"Because that they have forsaken me, and have worshipped Ashtoreth the goddess of the Zidonians, Chemosh the god of the Moabites, and Milcom the god of the children of Ammon, and have not walked in my ways, to do that which is right in mine eyes, and to keep my statutes and my judgments, as did David his father.

"Howbeit I will not take the whole kingdom out of his hand: but I will make him prince all the days of his life for David my servant's sake, whom I chose, because he kept my commandments and my statutes:

"But I will take the kingdom out of his son's hand, and will give it unto thee, even ten tribes.

"And unto his son will I give one tribe, that David my servant may have a light alway before me in Jerusalem, the city which I have chosen me to put my name there.

"And I will take thee, and thou shalt reign according to all that thy soul desireth, and shalt be king over Israel.

"And it shall be, if thou wilt hearken unto all that I command thee, and wilt walk in my ways, and do that is right in my sight, to keep my statutes and my commandments, as David my servant did; that I will be with thee, and build thee a sure house, as I built for David, and will give Israel unto thee.

"And I will for this afflict the seed of David, but not for ever."

   Murderous thoughts now entered the king's mind. How different was he at this point from Saul?

   "Solomon sought therefore to kill Jeroboam. And Jeroboam arose, and fled into Egypt, unto Shishak king of Egypt, and was in Egypt until the death of Solomon. . . .

   "And the time that Solomon reigned in Jerusalem over all Israel was forty years.

   "And Solomon slept with his fathers, and was buried in the city of David his father: and Rehoboam his son reigned in his stead." (1 Kings 11.)

Chapter Forty-four

SOLOMON'S PROVERBS

Solomon wrote 3,000 proverbs and 1,005 songs. (1 Kings 4:32.) They covered a wide range of subjects, far beyond those which are printed in our Bible.

The scripture says that he spake of trees, ''from the cedar tree that is in Lebanon even unto the hyssop that springeth out of the wall: he spake also of beasts, and of fowl, and of creeping things, and of fishes.'' (1 Kings 4:33.)

Those proverbs and songs that we have in our scriptures are highly inspirational. They cover a wide field, from the premortal existence to what the Lord hates, to instructions on rearing children, and finally to the ''conclusion of the whole matter.''

His discourse as descriptive of a premortal existence is one of the finest parts of his writings:

The Lord possessed me in the beginning of his way,

Before his works of old.

I was set up from everlasting,

From the beginning,

Or ever the earth was.

When there were no depths, I was brought forth;

When there were no fountains abounding with water.

Before the mountains were settled,

Before the hills was I brought forth:

While as yet he had not made the earth,

Nor the fields,

Nor the highest part of the dust of the world.

When he prepared the heavens, I was there:

When he set a compass upon the face

Of the depth:
When he established the clouds above:
When he strengthened the fountains
Of the deep:
When he gave to the sea his decree,
That the waters should not pass his commandment:
When he appointed the foundations of the earth:
Then I was by him,
As one brought up with him:
And I was daily his delight,
Rejoicing always before him.
(Proverbs 8:22-30.)

What the Lord hates is direct and certain:
These six things doth the Lord hate:
Yea, seven are an abomination unto him:
A proud look, a lying tongue,
And hands that shed innocent blood,
An heart that deviseth wicked imaginations,
Feet that be swift in running to mischief,
A false witness that speaketh lies,
And he that soweth discord among brethren.
(6:16-19.)

But then Solomon talks of obedience to the Lord:
My son, keep thy father's commandment,
And forsake not the law of thy mother:
Bind them continually upon thine heart,
And tie them about thy neck.
When thou goest, it shall lead thee;
When thou sleepest, it shall keep thee;
And when thou awakest, it shall talk with thee.
(6:20-22.)

His warning against evil women is this:

> For the commandment is a lamp;
> And the law is light;
> And reproofs of instruction are the way of life:
> To keep thee from the evil woman,
> From the flattery of the tongue
> Of a strange woman.
> Lust not after her beauty in thine heart;
> Neither let her take thee with her eyelids.
> For by means of a whorish woman
> A man is brought to a piece of bread:
> And the adulteress will hunt
> For the precious life.
> Can a man take fire in his bosom,
> And his clothes not be burned?
> Can one go upon hot coals,
> And his feet not be burned?
> So he that goeth in to his neighbour's wife;
> Whosoever toucheth her
> Shall not be innocent.
> Men do not despise a thief,
> If he steal to satisfy his soul
> When he is hungry;
> But if he be found,
> He shall restore sevenfold;
> He shall give all the substance of his house.
> But whoso committeth adultery with a woman
> Lacketh understanding:
> He that doeth it destroyeth his own soul.
> (6:23-32.)

One of the most eloquent and beloved expressions speaks of the virtuous woman:

Who can find a virtuous woman?
For her price is far above rubies.
The heart of her husband doth safely trust in her,
So that he shall have no need of spoil.
She will do him good and not evil
All the days of her life.
She seeketh wool, and flax,
And worketh willingly with her hands.
She is like the merchants' ships;
She bringeth her food from afar.
She riseth also while it is yet night,
And giveth meat to her household,
And a portion to her maidens.
She considereth a field, and buyeth it:
With the fruit of her hands
She planteth a vineyard.
She girdeth her loins with strength,
And strengtheneth her arms.
She perceiveth that her merchandise is good:
Her candle goeth not out by night.
She layeth her hands to the spindle,
And her hands hold the distaff.
She stretcheth out her hand to the poor;
Yea, she reacheth forth her hands to the needy.
She is not afraid of the snow for her household:
For all her household are clothed with scarlet.
She maketh herself coverings of tapestry;
Her clothing is silk and purple.
Her husband is known in the gates,
When he sitteth among the elders of the land.
She maketh fine linen, and selleth it;
And delivereth girdles unto the merchant.

Strength and honour are her clothing;

And she shall rejoice in time to come.

She openeth her mouth with wisdom;

And in her tongue is the law of kindness.

She looketh well to the ways of her household,

And eateth not the bread of idleness.

Her children arise up, and call her blessed;

Her husband also, and he praiseth her.

Many daughters have done virtuously,

But thou excellest them all.

Favour is deceitful, and beauty is vain:

But a woman that feareth the Lord,

She shall be praised.

Give her of the fruit of her hands;

And let her own works praise her in the gates.

(31:10-31.)

On the subject of training children Solomon speaks a good deal about proper discipline and says:

He that spareth his rod hateth his son:

But he that loveth him chasteneth him betimes. . . .

Chasten thy son while there is hope,

And let not thy soul spare for his crying. . . .

Train up a child in the way he should go:

And when he is old, he will not depart from it.

(13:24; 19:18; 22:6.)

And his advice to children:

My son, hear the instruction of thy father,

And forsake not the law of thy mother.

(1:8.)

Self-control is emphasized in a number of the proverbs. Among them are these:

He that is slow to wrath is of great understanding:

But he that is hasty of spirit exalteth folly. (14:29.)

A soft answer turneth away wrath:
But grievous words stir up anger. (15:1.)

He that is slow to anger is better than the mighty;
And he that ruleth his spirit
Than he that taketh a city. (16:32.)

Answer not a fool according to his folly,
Lest thou also be like unto him. (26:4.)

Faithful are the wounds of a friend;
But the kisses of an enemy are deceitful. (27:6.)
Solomon's regard for the poor is expressed this way:
He that hath pity upon the poor
Lendeth unto the Lord;
And that which he hath given
Will he pay him again. (19:7.)
And what did Solomon think of pride? He said:
Every one that is proud in heart
Is an abomination to the Lord:
Though hand join in hand,
He shall not be unpunished. (16:5.)

Pride goeth before destruction,
And an haughty spirit before a fall. (16:18.)

A good name is rather to be chosen
Than great riches,
And loving favour
Rather than silver and gold. (22:1.)

Among Solomon's choice bits in Ecclesiastes is this well-known one:
To every thing there is a season,
And a time to every purpose under the heaven:

A time to be born, and a time to die;
A time to plant, and a time to pluck up
That which is planted;
A time to kill, and a time to heal;
A time to break down,
And a time to build up;
A time to weep, and a time to laugh;
A time to mourn, and a time to dance;
A time to cast away stones,
And a time to gather stones together;
A time to embrace,
And a time to refrain from embracing;
A time to get, and a time to lose;
A time to keep, and a time to cast away;
A time to rend, and a time to sew;
A time to keep silence, and a time to speak;
A time to love, and a time to hate;
A time of war, and a time of peace.
(Ecclesiastes 3:1-8.)

Solomon's fear of the Lord was well said:

The fear of the Lord is the beginning of knowledge:
But fools despise wisdom and instruction. (Proverbs 1:7.)

And then he continues with these:

Trust in the Lord with all thine heart;
And lean not unto thine own understanding.
In all thy ways acknowledge him,
And he shall direct thy paths. (3:5-6.)
Honour the Lord with thy substance,
And with the firstfruits of all thine increase:
So shall thy barns be filled with plenty,
And thy presses shall burst out with new wine.
My son, despise not the chastening of the Lord;

Neither be weary of his correction:

For whom the Lord loveth he correcteth;

Even as a father the son

In whom he delighteth. (3:9-12.)

In the early days of his reign, when he was blessed abundantly with the Spirit of the Lord, Solomon spoke as a prophet, giving expression to these true teachings of the Lord. They were inspired, and they are scripture to us.

It was only in his later years, when the "strange women" led him into idolatry, that he lost the Spirit, and hence spoke no more wisdom.

While he served the Lord he was great—incomparable!

When he turned away, he became a heartbroken weakling.

Chapter Forty-five

THE FINAL LESSON

The lives of the three great kings of Israel teach one unforget-table and poignant lesson. It is summarized clearly in these words from Ecclesiastes:

"Let us hear the conclusion of the whole matter: Fear God, and keep his commandments: for this is the whole duty of man." (Ecclesiastes 12:13.)

The history of the world could have been—indeed would have been—entirely different had these three monarchs followed that teaching. They knew full well the right way to go. None of them sinned in ignorance. All of them sinned against the well-known laws of God.

The Lord had promised to make Israel the greatest of all the nations. He showed that he was prepared to do so, and he went far in that direction in Solomon's time. But Israel rejected this op-portunity.

In the lives of Saul and Solomon particularly is illustrated the truth of the Book of Mormon teaching that an evil king can truly lead his people into degradation.

Under Saul wickedness and idolatry spread, bringing captiv-ity and slavery.

Under Solomon, idolatry once abolished returned again. Once more the people suffered. The kingdom was split. Taxes were exhorbitant; sin was rampant; and idolatrous nations be-came the conquerors of Israel.

How similar is the history of the Israelites in Palestine to that of the Book of Mormon peoples.

The Jaredites brought on destruction by apostatizing from the way of the Lord.

The Nephites, even blessed as no people had ever been blessed for two hundred years after the appearance of the Savior, went down to total annihilation because of their rebellion against the Lord.

In the days of Joseph Smith, when the Lord was prepared to build his modern Zion in Jackson County, Missouri, sin raised the barrier. The Lord told the Prophet:

"Behold, I say unto you, there were jarrings, and contentions, and envyings, and strifes, and lustful and covetous desires among them; therefore by these things they polluted their inheritances.

"They were slow to hearken unto the voice of the Lord their God; therefore, the Lord their God is slow to hearken unto their prayers, to answer them in the day of their trouble.

"In the day of their peace they esteemed lightly my counsel; but, in the day of their trouble, of necessity they feel after me.

"Verily I say unto you, notwithstanding their sins, my bowels are filled with compassion towards them. I will not utterly cast them off; and in the day of wrath I will remember mercy." (D&C 101:6-9.)

It is the same in all ages. If the Lord's people will serve him, they will prosper in the land. If they draw away from the Lord, he refuses to bless them. They reap what they sow.

This is true with individuals as well as with nations. The way to peace, happiness, and prosperity is clearly drawn. As Solomon so truly said:

"Fear God, and keep his commandments: for this is the whole duty of man."

INDEX